THE COMPLETE BOOK OF PIZZA

By Louise Love

Illustrated by Barbara Hahn

sfs® sassafras press

Evanston, Illinois 60204

"WHEN THE MOON HITS YOUR EYE LIKE A BIG PIZZA PIE, THAT'S AMORE"

Sassafras Enterprises, Inc., P.O. Box 461, Evanston, Illinois 60204.

LIBRARY OF CONGRESS CATALOG CARD NUMBER: 80-51184
ISBN NUMBER: 0-930528-03-04

Twenty-First Printing   May 1998

The publisher wishes to acknowledge Jack Brooks and Harry Warren for use of the music and lyrics to "That's Amore" quoted this page. Copyright ©1953 by Paramount Music Corporation.

Cover Illustration by Pat Koeller.
Printing & Production by Marco-Gruen Printers.

INTRODUCTION

Pizza is unique - - American as apple pie, but savored the world over. Pizza is a food which has universal appeal. It is considered a fast food. junk food, kids' food, snack food, take-out food, and, as this book shows, gourmet food.

Despite the universal appeal of pizza, it has still not been accorded its proper place in the gourmet world of cooking. Cooking schools relegate pizza making to the kids' classes while the adults learn how to make pasta or quiche. This cookbook elevates the art of pizza making to the cordon bleu classification of the culinary arts.

Louise Love is a pizza lover. She lives in Evanston, Illinois with her husband and two daughters and is a candidate for a doctorate degree at Northwestern University. Her interest and enthusiasm in this project made it a pleasure to work with her; her pizzas made it a treat.

Steven Schwab
Publisher

ACKNOWLEDGEMENTS

One of the nice things about working on a pizza project is that everyone is willing to help. I have had priceless assistance from many people in all phases of writing this book; good friends and chance acquaintances have made suggestions and given me recipes to try out. Flocks of helpers have been on hand to sample the experiments.

First, I would like to thank Steven Schwab, whose inspiration and investment have kept the project afloat. I have enjoyed working with Barbara Hahn; her talent and expertise have brought life to these pages. Heidi Levin has given endless hours of editorial assistance. I am grateful for her painstaking efforts and dedication.

For advice, recipes and stoveside assistance, I owe Barbara Penner, Russell Reising, Michael Valente, Sharon Dixon, Kevin McMullen, Margy Robson, Stephanie Schwab, Katy Hart, Jill Rubinstein and Mary Nell Reck. For outstanding gastronomical assistance, my thanks to Melissa Hart, Diana Brown, Betsy Chestnut, Jeff Giles and those indefatigable epicures, Cathy Wickum and Ann Wickum.

I am greatly indebted to two wonderful friends whose contributions have been too numerous to itemize. Their constant help and support have made the writing of this book possible and even pleasurable: Alan Olken and Beth Hart.

THIS BOOK IS LOVINGLY DEDICATED TO ERNIE, SARAH AND MARY WHO ATE THE MOST PIZZA AND KEPT ME COMPANY IN THE KITCHEN.

TABLE OF CONTENTS

Page

I. **THE PIE THAT WON THE WEST -** 9
The Story of Pizza

II. **THE FLOUR FOUNDATION -** 13
Making the Dough

III. **SATURDAY NIGHT PIZZA -** 25
Traditional and Original Recipes

IV. **THE MORNING AFTER -** 43
Special Pizza for Sunday Brunch

V. **VARIATIONS ON A NEOPOLITAN THEME -** 53
Analogies to Pizza from Around the World

VI. **MUDPIES -** 71
Recipes for Kids

VII. **SUPERMARKET PIZZA -** 81
Making the Best of It

VIII. **THE WAVE OF THE FUTURE -** 89
Using the Little Helpers Mama Never Had:
Food Processor, Microwave and Convection Oven,
Freezer and Barbecue

IX. **TOOLS OF THE TRADE -** 95
Utensils for Pizza Making

X. **INDEX** 99

I

THE PIE THAT WON THE WEST

The Story of Pizza

Americans are fond of saying that pizza is not really an Italian dish. After all, we have adopted pizza, glorified it, and raised it to a place of honor in our national cuisine. Pizza is second only in the hearts (and stomachs) of Americans to the hamburger (another European import). Our love for pizza may be passionate, but it is still young compared to the long devotion that the Italians--and before them their Roman ancestors--have accorded this enduring dietary staple. The pizza, and its ancestor in the ancient world, has always been a "popular" dish in both senses of the word. That is, it is both well-liked and a dish "of the people." In the Roman Republic and the Roman Empire, pizza was eaten by the working man and his family. It was a thrifty and convenient meal for that large social class that could not spend hours at the table.

What is pizza but a plate of bread dough on which to put other good things to eat? Such a dish was a common breakfast food in ancient Rome. As soon as wheat was introduced to the Roman world from Greece, Romans began to start the day with pizza. The dough they used was leavened with yeast, but it did not include any oil. This left the crust crisp and tough. Tomatoes were unknown, but the Romans had leeks and garlic, olives and herbs. Any of these things might have been scattered on the dough to enhance the morning meal. If the citizen were lucky enough to have some fish or cheese on hand, these might have been included as well. This was the proto-pizza from which the modern pizza that we know and love, and claim as our own, evolved.

The influences that shaped the development of pizza cookery reflected the increased foreign traffic that brought novelties from the East and the West to the Mediterranean world.

From the East came mozzarella cheese. In the 7th century A.D., herds of water buffalo were imported from India to the Campagna region of what is now Italy. From the milk of these buffalo came the original mozzarella, and from their descendants authentic mozzarella is still made today--one of the distinguishing features of genuine Neopolitan pizza! What we buy as mozzarella in America is a low-fat product of cow's milk. We are obviously very happy with our own version of mozzarella, but we should keep in mind that the most authentic pizza can only be made where true mozzarella is available. It is a highly perishable item which undoubtedly accounts for its failure to reach our shores as an export item.

Fortunately, parmesan cheese is a long-lived food which can be exported and is available to us in all its native glory. It has been made in and around Parma in the Reggio-Emilia region of Italy since at least the 10th century A.D. and has been prized for its seasoning qualities for as long as it has been made.

The West made its contribution to pizza, too. The Spanish conquistadores returned from Mexico with an exotic plant (a relative of the deadly nightshade) which bore bright red or golden fruit. It was called "pomodoro," golden apple, and "pomme d'amour," love apple; but no one would eat the fruit because it was believed to be poisonous. At first, the plants were introduced to Europe as a curiosity and as a decorative plant. Eventually, of course, the fruit was sampled, its good name was rescued, and cooks began to investigate its culinary potential. By the late 17th century, the cultivation of tomatoes for food was a thriving enterprise around Naples.

The classic combination which distinguishes Neopolitan pizza (mozzarella cheese, parmesan cheese and fresh, red tomatoes), was given the royal stamp of approval in 1889. King Umberto and his consort, Queen Margherita, were visiting Naples that year. They invited the renowned chef, Esposito, to prepare pizza for them during their stay. He presented the royal pair with several varieties of the local dish, and Margherita chose the tomato and cheese combination as her favorite. The dish was given her name; it became the basis for countless other variations. This queen was just one of many crowned heads in Europe who demonstrated a fondness of pizza.

Queen Maria Carolina was at least as fond of pizza as Queen Margherita. Her passion for pizza led her husband, Ferdinand I of Naples, to have royal pizza ovens built for her. Among her guests were Lord Nelson and Lady Hamilton, who journeyed to Italy to savor their favorite dish.

Armies as well as nobility spread the fame of pizza through Europe. The Roman army brought the recipe for pizza with onions, olives, and anchovies into France. The dish became naturalized into provincial cooking and is still served in southern France under the name, pissaladiere.

It was the movement of another, much later, army that led to the exportation and naturalization of Neopolitan pizza. Although the first pizzerias appeared in America in the 19th century when people began to leave Naples in search of livelihood in the New World, it was not until World War II that pizza began to catch on as a major American food. With the stationing of American soldiers in Italy came a growing appreciation of the joys of pizza served bubbling hot from the ancient ovens of Italy. When the G.I.'s returned to the United States, the demand for pizza at home began to grow. Supply followed demand as America's appetite for pizza continued to grow.

The pizza business is now estimated to be a $6,000,000,000 industry in the United States. Yet, in 1948 when *Time* magazine ran an article on the opera singer, Salvatore Baccaloni, which included the fact that he enjoyed pizza, the writer included a description so his national readership would know what he meant by pizza!

When American troops crowded the streets of Rome following World War II, the Santerini family made its fortune and reputation by inventing the capricciosa pizza. They thought of dividing the pizza into four sections, separated by strips of anchovy, and featuring a different topping on each of the four sections. This was the beginning of another pizza tradition--the partitioning of one pie into quadrants on which each diner gets to have the garnish of his choice.

Another part of the pizza tradition is "ordering out." Even in Naples, families will order out to the local pizzeria for an evening meal. This custom may work better there than it does here because the neighborhood pizzeria is never more than a few minutes away. The hour that elapses for us between the ordering of the pizza and its arrival can mean the sacrifice of the pizza's moment of perfection.

There is no question but that the best way to enjoy pizza in America is to make it yourself at home. There are things you can do to make your pizza much like the pizza of Naples. In the first place, you can line your oven with baking tiles and bake the pizza directly on them. The Neopolitans claim that the best pizza is made in an oven of brick or tile heated by a fire of hickory branches. To approximate the flavor and consistency of genuine buffalo-milk mozzarella, I follow a suggestion by Marcella Hazan in her authoritative book on Italian cooking. Soak grated mozzarella in olive oil for an hour before using it. Use three tablespoons of olive oil for every six ounces of cheese.

A homemade pizza is a thing of beauty. It may seem complicated the first time you make one, but it becomes very easy after you have made two or three. There is room for unlimited inventiveness in combining ingredients. A pizza can be designed for any taste.

If Americans err in claiming pizza as an American dish, they also err in thinking of pizza as "junk food." Perhaps it is a survival of the Puritan mentality that makes us feel that anything that tastes good can't possibly be good for us. The clincher in classifying pizza as junk food is the damning fact that kids like it. Furthermore, pizza is considered fattening. Once again, pizza is unfairly vilified because of its virtues. Pizza tastes so good that we tend to eat too much of it. **Then,** it becomes fattening. If you eat pizza as moderately as you eat, say, calves' liver, it is not fattening. As a final irrefutable testament to the virtues of pizza, I give you the United States Department of Agriculture's breakdown of the caloric and nutritional values of pizza. The information given is for a slice of homemade cheese pizza (one-eighth of the pie) that is 12" in diameter, made with unbleached all-purpose white flour and vegetable oil.†

Calories	145
Protein	6 gm.
Fat	4 gm.
Carbohydrate	22 gm.
Calcium	86 mg.
Phosphorus	89 mg.

Iron	1.1 mg.
Potassium	67 mg.
Vitamin A	230 I.U.
Ascorbic Acid (Vit. C)	4 mg.
Thiamine	.16 mg.
Niacin	1.6 mg.
Riboflavin	.18 mg.

To get the full nutritional value from your homemade pizza, use only fresh ingredients--and buy the best. Economize anywhere but on the food you eat. Be ready, also, to spend some time in the kitchen. This should be pleasurable, creative time. Preparing food is a life-sustaining activity and should be approached with seriousness of purpose as well as delight. A Frenchman once said, "In the kitchen, more than anywhere, nothing leads to nothing." Putting his sentiment more positively: If you want something good to come out of the oven, you've got to put something good into it.

† Home and Garden Bulletin #72, 1977.

II

THE FLOUR FOUNDATION

Making the Dough

A good dough is the basis of a flavorful and well-textured crust. Homemade pizza dough is fundamentally the same as bread dough. The timing of pizza dough is not as involved as bread dough, however, because for most pizza recipes the dough only has to rise once for about an hour and a half. After this single rising period, you can roll out the dough and bake your pizza. If you are an experienced bread-maker, you know how easy it is to manage the ingredients and the timing of a yeast-risen dough. If you have never made a yeast dough before, it may seem difficult when you read about it, but be assured it is not. Like anything else, experience leads to confidence. With a little practice, anyone can become a confident dough maker and learn to enjoy the various steps necessary for the creation of a perfect crust.

Once you have mastered the basic method for making pizza dough, you might want to create new doughs of your own invention. If you maintain the proportion of liquid to dry ingredients and keep in mind the conditions under which the yeast will do its work, you can change the ingredients to suit your own palate and diet. You are in control.

In this chapter, I have included several classic dough recipes and some variations. These are only a few of the many possibilities--let your inspiration be your guide and experiment freely.

When I have dough left over after making pizza, I make it into bread or rolls. All you have to do is gather the leftover dough into a ball and put it back in a warm, draft-free place for 40 minutes so it will rise again. Then shape it into a loaf or individual rolls, cover and let rise again for another 40 minutes. Then pop it into a 375° oven and bake it until it is golden brown. The cooking time will depend, in part, on the size of your loaf. You can also wrap leftover dough tightly and keep it in the refrigerator for use the following day or freeze it.

BASIC PIZZA DOUGH

This dough makes a delicious and versatile crust. It can be thin and crisp or thick and chewy, depending on how it is rolled out and baked. After the recipe, I have given instructions on preparing the various kinds of pizzas from this dough. All of the recipes that are given on the following pages make doughs that can be prepared in any of these styles. The individual recipes will tell you how to put the pizzas together after the dough has risen. This recipe will make:

2 thin crust pizzas, 12" each
2 stuffed pizza pockets
1 thick crust pizza, 14"
1 Chicago-style deep dish pizza, 13" to 14"
6 individual pizzas, 6" each
25 individual calzones

Ingredients
4½ cups	unbleached all-purpose white flour
1 tsp.	salt
¼ cup (4 tbsp.)	olive oil
2 pkgs.	dry yeast
1½ cups	warm water
2 tsp.	light brown sugar

Measure ½ cup warm water (about 110°) in a measuring cup and stir in 2 tsp. of light brown sugar. Be sure the water is only warm--not hot. If the water is too hot, it will kill the yeast and the dough will not rise. The warm water and the sugar help the yeast to become active. Dissolve the 2 packages of yeast in the water and set it aside for at least 5 minutes. The yeast will become frothy during this time.

Meanwhile, sift 4 cups of flour into a large mixing bowl with the salt. Make a depression in the middle of the flour and add 3 tbsp. of olive oil and 1 cup of warm water. When the yeast mixture has risen for 5 minutes, add it to the flour.

Dust the surface on which you will be kneading the dough with flour. Now mix all of the ingredients in the bowl with your hands and gather them together and place them on the floured board. Knead the dough for 8 to 10 minutes.

Knead the dough by pushing part of it away from you with the heel of one hand and then folding it back towards you. Repeat with the heel of the other hand. Then rotate the dough ¼ turn and repeat. Add more flour to the board (it will become incorporated into the dough) if the mixture is too wet or too sticky. Eventually the dough will become elastic and will stay together in a cohesive ball.

Rub a clean bowl with olive oil and place the kneaded dough in it. Moisten the top of the dough with oil as well. Place a clean dish towel over the bowl and put it in a warm, draft-free place to rise. The oven is a perfect place to let the dough rise. The pilot light generates a little warmth and there are no drafts to disturb the dough. However, if you're using the oven for

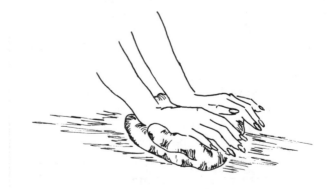

something else, a cleared space in your linen closet is a good alternative as a warm, draft-free location for rising dough.

When the dough has risen for 1½ hours, remove it and place it again on the floured board. You are now ready to roll out the dough for the pizza of your choice.

USING THE DOUGH
The Varieties of Pizza

Thin-Crust Pizza: The recipe given above will make two, 12″ thin-crust pizzas. Preheat the oven to 500°. Divide the dough into equal balls. With your hand, flatten each ball into a circle. Put flour on a board and on your rolling pin. Roll the circle flat until it is somewhat larger than your pizza pan. You will probably have to sprinkle flour on the dough from time to time to keep it from sticking to the rolling pin. Rotate the dough occasionally as you roll it out. You should also lift the dough up carefully at least once, place more flour on the board, and turn the dough over to roll the other side.

As you become more expert, you will be able to throw the dough over your head, as you have seen chefs do in pizzerias. It may take you a little while, however, to build up the confidence to try this. If the dough gets out of shape and you cannot restore the circle (or approximate circle), you can always gather it back into a ball and start again. If you do not have a pizza pan and are using a rectangular cookie sheet instead, roll the dough into an oblong shape that more nearly conforms to the dimensions of your pan.

When the dough has been rolled out, sprinkle a little cornmeal on your pizza pan, pie pan or cookie sheet and lift the dough carefully so you can slip the pan under it. The dough should hang over the edge of the pan all around. Roll up the edge of the dough to form a rim that will

hold in the sauce and the cheese. You can make a very attractive rim by lifting the dough over your finger to form pleats. Brush the dough with a little olive oil before putting the sauce on it. This will help prevent sogginess. Thin-crust pizzas take from 10 to 15 minutes to bake at 500°. Oven temperatures vary, so you should judge the baking time of your pizza by the look of the crust and the filling. The crust should be golden brown and crisp looking; the filling should be bubbling and the cheese melted but not toasting when the pizza is done. You will come to know what to expect of your own oven by experience.

A thin-crust pizza can be made without a pizza pan directly on baking tiles or a pizza stone. This method yields the best crust possible, reproducing the virtues of a stone oven. If you have such a stone or tiles, be sure that you preheat them in the oven for a half hour. Sprinkle cornmeal on them shortly before you are ready to bake the pizza. Assemble the pizza on a pizza paddle (peel) that has also been sprinkled with cornmeal. The cornmeal allows the pizza to slide off of the paddle and onto the stone easily.

When you are making a pizza without a pan, let the dough rise for a little while after you have rolled it out and formed the rim. This will give you a better foundation for holding in the filling ingredients. When you have the dough assembled on the pizza peel, brush the bottom, but not the rim of the pizza, with olive oil. Cover with a clean cloth and put in a warm place for 15 to 20 minutes. After the dough has risen slightly, brush the rim with oil and proceed to fill and bake.

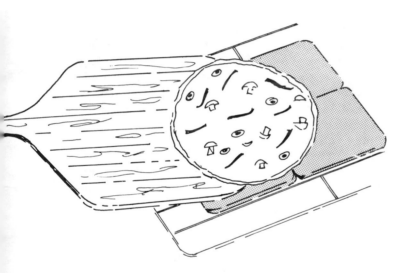

Stuffed Pizza Pocket: The Basic Pizza Dough recipe will make two stuffed pizza pockets. Preheat the oven to 400°. Divide the dough into two equal balls. Roll out the dough as if you were making 12" thin-crust pizzas. When the dough is ready, sprinkle cornmeal on your baking pan and slip the dough onto it. Place the filling on one half of the dough. Dip your finger in a glass of water and moisten the entire edge of the dough, then fold the unfilled half of the dough over the filling. Roll up the edges of the dough and seal it together by pressing down on it with your fingers. Make three little cuts in the top of the dough to allow steam to escape during the baking process. Repeat for the second ball of dough. You will probably want to use a different filling for each of the stuffed pizzas. You may bake them on cookie sheets, a pizza pan, pie pans, or baking stone. Stuffed pizzas look very pretty when they are glazed before baking with a mixture of egg yolk and olive oil. Baking time is about 35 minutes or until golden brown.

You can make one large circular stuffed pizza instead of two semi-circular pockets. To do this, simply roll out both balls of dough to approximately the same size (about 12" each). Brush one with olive oil and spread the filling over it, leaving a rim of about an inch all around. Place the second crust on top of the filling and roll the lower crust over the upper crust, forming a sealed rim. Pierce the crust with a sharp knife and glaze it with the egg yolk and olive oil mixture. Bake for about 35 minutes at 400°.

Thick-Crust Pizza: The Basic Pizza Dough recipe will make one, 14" thick crust pizza. After the dough has risen for an hour, punch it down and let it stand for a second hour. Then preheat your oven to 350° and roll out the dough and place it on the pan, making a rim around the edge by rolling up the dough with your fingers. Allow the dough to rise in the pan for 15 minutes and then place it in the oven for 10 minutes unfilled. Remove the partially baked crust from the oven and assemble the filling on it. Complete the baking for another 20 minutes or until the crust is golden brown and the filling is bubbly.

Chicago-Style Deep Dish Pizza: The Basic Pizza Dough recipe will make one, 13" Chicago-style deep dish pizza. Preheat the oven to 450°. Sprinkle a little cornmeal in the bottom of the deep dish pizza pan. Place the ball of dough on the floured board and flatten the ball into a circle with your hand. Put flour on the dough and on the rolling pin and roll it out to a circle which is larger than the pan. While you are rolling out the dough, rotate it and turn it over, reflouring the board from time to time. When the circle is about 17" across, slip it over the pan and press the dough against the sides. Brush the dough with olive oil and assemble the pizza. This type of pizza will take about 25 minutes to cook. The crust should be golden brown and the filling bubbly.

Chicago-Style Deep Dish Double-Crust Pizza: To make one, 13"-14" double-crust pizza you will need to make one and a half times the Basic Pizza Dough recipe. This method differs from a circular stuffed pizza in that it has two layers of filling as well as two crusts. The dough must be rolled very thin for this creation.

Preheat the oven to 500°. Divide the dough into two equal parts. Roll out one part of the dough until it is at least 17" in diameter. Sprinkle a little cornmeal into a deep dish pizza pan and slip the dough over the pan. Press the edges of the dough against the pan. The dough should still partially overhang the pan. Brush the dough with olive oil. Place mozzarella cheese and filling ingredients on the dough.

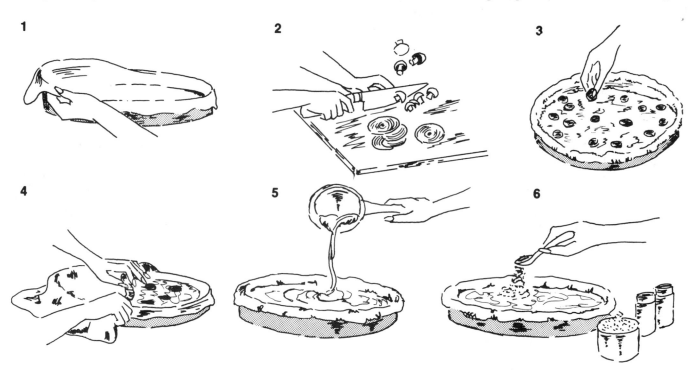

Delicate ingredients, such as seafood and thinly sliced vegetables, will preserve their moisture in this layer. However, reserve the sauce for the top crust. Roll out the second ball of dough and place it over the first layer. Crimp the edges of the dough together with your fingers. Brush the second layer with olive oil. Spread tomato sauce, mozzarella, parmesan over the top layer. Bake for about 25 minutes or until the crust is done. Allow the double-crust pizza to cool for a few minutes before cutting.

Individual Pizzas: The Basic Pizza Dough recipe will make six individual 6" pizzas. Preheat the oven to 500°. Divide the dough into six equal balls. Sprinkle cornmeal on your baking surface. You may use cookie sheets, baking tiles or pizza pans for baking these small pizzas. Roll out each dough ball to a 7" to 8" diameter. Lift the dough onto the baking surface and roll up the edge all around to make a rim. Repeat the process for each of the six balls of dough. When the individual pies are ready, brush each of them with olive oil and fill for baking. Baking time should be about 10 minutes or until the crust is golden brown.

Individual Deep-Fried Calzone: The Basic Pizza Dough recipe will make 25 individual calzones. In a very large pot or frying pan place two inches of good cooking oil. Heat the oil while you are preparing the calzone, but do not let it smoke. Take a small piece of the dough and place it in the oil once it has started to heat so that you may judge when it is ready to deep fry the calzone. You will know it is ready when the piece of dough is sizzling quietly in the oil. It should be turning golden brown. If the oil gets too hot, turn the heat off and let it cool. You may then start reheating it more gently.

Use a dough cutter or any circular object that you can use to cut dough with a diameter of about four inches. I use a large drinking glass. You may want to dip the cutting edge in flour to make cleaner cuts. Roll out the dough as if you were going to make thin-crust pizza and use your cutter to make circles from the dough. Fill one side of the circle with the filling of your choice. Dip your finger in a glass of water and moisten the edges of the little circles. Then lift the unfilled portion of the dough over the filling and seal the edges together. You will have a tiny stuffed pizza that looks like a homemade ravioli. Repeat this process until all of the dough is gone. You can put various fillings in the calzones to suit the tastes of those who will be eating them. If the oil is hot enough, you may want to start frying the first few while you are making others. This job is easier if two people work on it together.

To fry the calzones, just drop them into the hot oil. They should swell up and begin to brown immediately. Gently turn them over in the oil with tongs. They will take only three or four minutes to cook. When they are nicely browned on both sides, take them out of the oil and drain on paper for a minute. The inside will be burning hot when they first come out of the oil, so restrain yourself from biting right in. Let them cool for a minute or two before cautiously having your first taste. These little treats look wonderfully festive and are delicious. I have never known anyone who did not rave about them. You can experiment with fillings to create your own favorite.

A FINAL WORD ON CRUSTS

Neopolitan bakers and American experts agree that the best crusts, for both bread and pizza, are baked in brick ovens. The advantages of these ovens can be recreated to some extent by placing either baking tiles or a baking stone in your oven. These tiles create an even temperature in the oven. Furthermore, if you bake directly on unglazed tiles, they will absorb moisture in a way that improves the quality of your crusts. These tiles are available in gourmet shops and in many gourmet mail-order catalogues.

You may bake directly on the tiles or in a baking pan placed on top of the tiles. Some people use quarry tiles or other bricks to create the effect of a brick oven. If you decide to use something in your oven that is not manufactured specifically for cooking purposes, be sure to find out whether any toxic material has been used in its manufacture. Tell the person from whom you buy it that you intend to use it for cooking.

For the optimum results with a baking stone or baking tiles, preheat them in the oven for a half hour before you are ready to bake. If you bake directly on the stone, sprinkle cornmeal on it before you slide the pizza or bread dough onto it. Remember that the stone will retain heat for a long time. Be sure to use a pot holder when you remove a stone from the oven unless it has had a long time to cool down.

WHOLE WHEAT PIZZA DOUGH

If you use all whole wheat, as this recipe suggests, you will have a hearty whole wheat flavor. You may substitute part white flour if you prefer a lighter whole wheat flavor. This recipe will make the same number of pizzas as the Basic Pizza Dough recipe.

4 cups	whole wheat flour
1 tsp.	salt
¼ cup (4 tbsp.)	safflower oil
2 pkgs.	dry yeast
2 tsp.	honey
1½ cups	warm water

Dissolve the yeast in ½ cup warm (not hot) water and add 2 tsp. of honey. Set aside for at least 5 minutes. Meanwhile, sift the flour and salt into a bowl. Make a depression in the center of the flour and add 3 tbsp. of the oil and the other cup of warm water. Put flour on a kneading board. Add the yeast mixture to the flour and mix the ingredients with your hands. Gather the dough together and place it on the floured board. Knead the dough, adding more flour if necessary. Knead for 8 to 10 minutes. The dough should be elastic and cohesive.

Place the dough in a clean bowl that has been rubbed with oil. Brush the top of the dough with the remaining oil. Cover the bowl with a clean towel and put it in a warm, draft-free place for 1½ hours.

SPINACH AND RICOTTA PIZZA DOUGH

This is a pretty-looking dough and a good way to get spinach into the kids. The spinach flavor is very mild and the color is a healthy green. A good pizza for a Christmas party could be made from this green crust with a bright red tomato filling. This recipe will make the same number of pizzas as the Basic Pizza Dough recipe.

1 cup	fresh spinach leaves lightly steamed
1 cup	ricotta cheese
1 egg	
4½ cups	unbleached all-purpose white flour
1 tsp.	salt
¼ cup (4 tbsp.)	olive oil
2 pkgs.	dry yeast
2 tsp.	light brown sugar
¾ cup	warm water

Dissolve the yeast in the warm water and stir in the light brown sugar. Set the yeast mixture aside for at least 5 minutes. Meanwhile, put the ricotta cheese and the spinach leaves in a blender and blend at high speed until you have a smooth, bright green mixture. Sift the flour into a bowl with the salt. Make a depression in the center of the flour and add 3 tbsp. of the oil, the egg, the spinach mixture and the yeast mixture. Put flour on the kneading board and place the dough mixture on the flour. Knead the mixture for 8 to 10 minutes until the dough is uniformly mixed and elastic. Add flour as you knead if necessary to keep the dough from becoming too sticky. When the dough is ready, place it in a clean bowl that has been brushed with oil. Brush the top of the dough with oil and place a clean cloth over the bowl. Put the bowl in a warm, draft-free place for 1½ hours.

RYE PIZZA DOUGH

This dough has a very light rye flavor. You may increase the rye flavor if you wish to by increasing the ratio of rye to white flour and by adding caraway seeds to the dough. This recipe will make the same number of pizzas as the Basic Pizza Dough recipe.

2 cups	rye flour
2½ cups	unbleached all-purpose white flour
1 tsp.	salt
¼ cup (4 tbsp.)	olive oil
2 pkgs.	dry yeast
1½ cups	warm water
2 tsp.	light brown sugar

Dissolve the yeast in ½ cup of warm water and stir in the light brown sugar. Set this mixture aside and let it stand for at least 5 minutes. Meanwhile, sift the rye flour and 2 cups of the white flour into a large mixing bowl with the salt. Make a depression in the center of the flour and add 3 tbsp. of the oil and 1 cup of warm water. Add the yeast mixture, mixing the dough with your hands. Place flour on the kneading surface and lift the dough onto it. Knead for 8 to 10 minutes. Place the dough in a clean bowl that has been brushed with oil. Brush the top of the dough with oil. Put a clean cloth over the bowl and put it in a warm, draft-free place for 1½ hours.

BUTTERMILK PIZZA DOUGH

The flavor of this dough is faintly cheesie and the texture softer than most doughs. If you like a less chewy crust, you will enjoy this one. This recipe will make the same number of pizzas as the Basic Pizza Dough recipe.

4-5 cups	unbleached all-purpose flour
1½ cups	buttermilk
½ cup (¼ lb.)	butter
3 tbsp.	light brown sugar
1 tsp.	salt
½ tsp.	baking powder
½ cup	water
1 tbsp.	vegetable oil
2 pkgs.	dry yeast

Put the butter and the buttermilk in a saucepan and place it over a low flame. Warm the milk slowly so the butter melts in it. Do not let the milk get hot. Stir the yeast and sugar into ½ cup of warm water. Let stand for 5 minutes. Sift 4 cups of flour, the salt, and baking powder into a large bowl. Stir in the warm milk and melted butter. Add the yeast mixture. Mix the ingredients thoroughly in the bowl and then turn them out onto a floured board. Knead for 8 minutes, incorporating more flour into the dough if necessary to keep it from being too sticky. When the dough has reached a smooth consistency, put it in a clean bowl and brush vegetable oil over the top of the dough. Cover with a clean towel and place in a warm, draft-free place for 1½ hours.

CHEESE AND ONION PIZZA DOUGH

This dough is especially good for stuffed pizza and deep-fried calzone, although you will also like it for your regular pizzas. You might want to experiment with various herbs in this dough in addition to the cheese and onions--oregano, basil, tarragon, fennel, whatever you like best. Be sure, however, that you grind the dried leaves to a powder with a mortar and pestle before adding them to the dough so that you will get an over-all subtle herb flavoring. Two teaspoons of pulverized herbs will be plenty. This recipe will make the same number of pizzas as the Basic Pizza Dough recipe.

4½ cups	unbleached all-purpose white flour
1 tsp.	salt
¼ cup (4 tbsp.)	olive oil
2 pkgs.	dry yeast
2 tsp.	light brown sugar
1 cup	warm water
1 egg	
⅔ cup	finely chopped onion
⅔ cup	freshly grated parmesan cheese

Dissolve the yeast in the warm water and stir in the light brown sugar. Set this mixture aside and let it stand for at least 5 minutes. Meanwhile, sift 4 cups of flour into a large mixing bowl with the salt. Make a depression in the center of the flour and add the onions, cheese, egg, 3 tbsp. of the olive oil and the yeast mixture. Put flour on the kneading surface. Mix the dough together with your hands and lift it onto the kneading surface. Knead for 8 to 10 minutes, then place the dough into a clean bowl that has been brushed with oil. Brush the top of the dough with oil. Put a clean cloth over the bowl and put it in a warm, draft-free place for 1½ hours.

SLOW-RISING PIZZA DOUGH

This is a delicious, moist and chewy dough that can be reheated successfully. The dough must rise for at least 3 hours, but it improves if it is left for more than 6 hours. This property should be an advantage to the working person who would like to prepare the dough in the morning and forget about it until he or she returns home in the evening. It is quicker to make homemade pizza than it is to order out when the dough is ready to roll. This recipe will make the same number of pizzas as the Basic Pizza Dough recipe.

2	potatoes (peeled)
5 cups	unbleached all-purpose white flour
1 cup	milk
1 cup	water
2 tbsp.	olive oil
1 tsp.	salt

Boil the potatoes until they are easily pierced by a fork. Let them cool, then mash them or put them through a food mill or a ricer. Sift 4½ cups of the flour into a bowl. Add the salt, milk, water, 1 tbsp. of oil and 1 cup of mashed potatoes. Knead the dough for 8 to 10 minutes, adding flour if the dough is too sticky. Place the dough in a clean bowl that has been brushed with oil. Sprinkle some flour on the top of the dough and brush with a little oil. Place a cloth over the bowl and put it in a warm place for 3 to 8 hours. The dough will rise slowly. If you use it after 3 hours, it will be very soft. You might have to press it into the pizza shape instead of rolling it. After about 5 hours, however, it should be very elastic and can be rolled thin.

BAKING SODA PIZZA DOUGH

You do not have to let this dough rise. You can, therefore, make a pizza on the spur of the moment. The crust has a soda-biscuit flavor and texture, but not the chewy breadlike pizza crust that is usual. You may find that children are partial to this crust. It is a good dough for them to start with when they want to make pizza because of the shortened time needed to complete the task.

The dough is soft and not as elastic as a yeast risen dough. You may have to press it into shape instead of rolling it with a rolling pin. If you tear a hole in the dough while you are pressing it out, you can repair it easily by closing the hole and pinching the dough together with your fingers. For one 14" pizza.

2 cups	unbleached all-purpose white flour
1 tsp.	salt
2 tbsp.	baking powder
½ cup (8 tbsp.)	olive oil
⅔ cup	water

Preheat the oven to 450°.
Sift the dry ingredients into a bowl, then add the water, and 6 tbsp. of the olive oil. Mix the ingredients together with your hands and then turn them out onto a floured kneading board. Knead for 2 minutes and place the ball of dough onto your baking surface which has been sprinkled with flour. Press the dough into a flat circle, repairing any tears in the dough as you go along. The circle of dough should be slightly larger than the final pizza will be. Roll up the edges of the dough to make a rim. Brush the dough with the remaining olive oil. You are now ready to assemble your pizza and bake for 15 minutes.

BRIOCHE PIZZA DOUGH

This is a rich dough that could be used for pastry. It makes a wonderful crust for a savory pizza and can be used for dessert pizzas as well (see Apple and Cheddar Pizza p. 48). Be sure that you glaze the dough before baking and keep an eye on it in the oven. It is more delicate than the other pizza doughs and more apt to burn. This recipe is for one 12" pizza.

3 cups	unbleached all-purpose flour
½ tsp.	salt
¼ cup	butter
½ cup	milk
2 eggs	
1 pkg.	dry yeast
¼ cup	warm water
2 tbsp.	light brown sugar

Dissolve the yeast in the warm water and add the sugar. Set the yeast mixture aside for at least 5 minutes. In a small saucepan gently heat the milk and the butter together until the butter is melted. Do not let the milk boil. Sift 2½ cups of the flour into a large bowl. Add the salt, eggs, milk and butter and the yeast mixture. Mix the ingredients together with a wooden spoon and turn them out onto a floured board. Knead the dough, adding more flour if necessary for 8 to 10 minutes. Gather the dough into a smooth ball and place it in a lightly oiled mixing bowl. Brush the top of the dough with oil. Cover the bowl with a clean cloth and place it in a warm, draft-free place for 2 hours.

PITA BREAD

Pita bread originated in the Middle East. It has a hollow pocket inside that can be stuffed with good things to eat. The Israelis have adopted pita for use with felafel, and more and more Americans are buying it to make sandwiches, hors d'oeuvres, and pizzas.

These flat, round loaves are available frozen in many supermarkets, but you will have a good time making them at home. The rising time for pita is considerably longer than for pizza as it has to go through several rising periods. Be sure the oven is thoroughly preheated before you put the loaves in. The very hot oven makes the dough pop up and form the empty pocket inside. For eight pita breads.

2 cups	unbleached all-purpose white flour
1 pkg.	dry yeast
1 tsp.	salt
1 tsp.	sugar
¾ cup	luke warm water

Dissolve the yeast and sugar in the warm water and set aside for 5 minutes. Sift the flour and salt into a bowl. Make a depression in the flour and pour in the yeast mixture. Mix well and turn out onto a floured board. Knead the dough for 8 to 10 minutes.

Dust the top of the dough with flour and place it in a clean bowl, cover with a clean dish towel and set it in a warm, draft-free place to rise for 1½ hours. Punch the dough down and let it rise for another 45 minutes.

After the second rising period, knead the dough for 2 minutes and form it into 8 balls of equal size. Cover the balls and let them rise for another half hour. Preheat the oven for 15 minutes to 500° (or the highest setting your oven has). After they have risen, flatten the dough balls with the palm of your hand. They should be about ¼" thick. Lightly flour a baking sheet and bake 1 or 2 of the pieces of dough at a time for 3 to 4 minutes on each side.

Pita will be light brown in color when it is done. The loaves will puff as they bake.

PUMPERNICKEL PIZZA DOUGH

Try this dough with Deli Pizza, p. 34, or Pizza Smorgasbord, p. 49. This recipe will make the same number of pizzas as the Basic Pizza Dough recipe.

3 cups	rye flour
2 cups	white flour
1½ tsp.	salt
¼ cup (4 tbsp.)	olive oil
½ cup	molasses
2 pkgs.	yeast
1½ cups	warm water
1 tsp.	light brown sugar

Dissolve the yeast with the sugar in ½ cup of warm water. Set aside for at least 5 minutes. Sift the rye flour and 1½ cups of the white flour together with the salt in a large bowl. Add the olive oil, the molasses, 1 cup of warm water and the yeast mixture. Mix the ingredients together with your hands and lift them onto a well-floured (white flour) board. Knead the dough for about 10 minutes, incorporating more flour if necessary to keep the dough from being too sticky. Place the dough in a clean bowl that has been brushed with oil. Brush the dough with oil, cover and place in a warm, draft-free place for 1½ hours.

III

SATURDAY NIGHT PIZZA

Traditional and Original Recipes

You have to make some decisions before you can make pizza. After you have made a choice between one large pizza or several small ones, thick crust or thin crust, flat pizza or stuffed pizza, you will have to decide on the ingredients that you want to use to fill the crust. For most pizzas you will want to have a well-seasoned tomato sauce. Neopolitan pizza often features fresh tomatoes instead of the sauce that is customary on American pizzas. Try sliced or chopped fresh tomatoes instead of sauce in the summer when you can get dead-ripe tomatoes. You may use Italian plum tomatoes or American slicing tomatoes when you are slicing them fresh; for sauce, however, use only Italian plum tomatoes. American slicing tomatoes are very juicy and make a thin and watery sauce. Drain the liquid from the fresh slices when you use them to prevent your crust from becoming soggy. When you use sauce, your seasonings are generally included in it and need not be added to the pizza again. When you use fresh tomatoes, however, you must season the pizza with oregano, salt, pepper, basil, garlic or other seasonings you like.

Assembling the Pizza

When your dough has risen once and the sauce is ready, you can put your pizza together. Be sure the oven is preheating to the proper temperature while you are building the pizza.

Using a pastry brush or piece of paper, brush the dough with olive oil after you have rolled it out and turned up the edge to form a rim. Spoon sauce onto the pizza to cover the whole surface, using the back of a spoon to spread the sauce evenly. Distribute the other ingredients that you have decided upon over the sauce. Some favorite additions are: sliced green pepper, sliced mushrooms (these may be sauteed in advance if you prefer), sliced onion, crumbled bacon, pepperoni, sausage (pre-cooked), capers, olives, anchovies, hard-boiled egg, raw vegetables, shrimp (pre-cooked), mussels, ground beef (pre-cooked).

Now add mozzarella and grated parmesan or romano cheese to the top. The mozzarella cheese may be sliced thin or grated. It is easier to spread the cheese evenly if it is grated. The amount of cheese you use depends upon your taste. Most of my friends like quite a lot of melted cheese. Use at least a cup of grated mozzarella and a quarter cup of grated parmesan for a 12" pizza. Dribble olive oil over the top of the pizza and place in the pre-heated oven. When it is done, remove from the oven and serve while it is still bubbling. Don't burn your mouth, but eat the pizza while it is still hot. There may be some who fancy warm, cold and reheated pizza; but not I. Pizza reaches its peak of perfection while it is still only minutes out of the oven.

It is good advice in general for cooks to use only the freshest and best ingredients. I cannot emphasize this too strongly for pizza. The olive oil should be a delicately flavored first or second pressing oil. You can get an idea of the delicacy of the oil by its color: it should not be too dark. Generally, the darker the color of the oil, the greater the number of pressings the olives have been through. Filippo Berio is an excellent brand of oil and so is Bertoli. If you have to hunt around to find a good Italian oil in your neighborhood, so much greater the adventure. You may discover all kinds of wonderful things while looking for olive oil. Think of what Columbus discovered trying to find the spices of the orient.

Parmesan cheese must, by all means, be freshly grated. The flavor, texture, and meltability of freshly grated parmesan is so far superior to the pre-grated cheese that comes in a box or a jar that they really cannot be thought of as the same thing. You cannot substitute one for the other and get the same results. You will find, too, that you pay a lot for the privilege of not grating your own cheese in money as well as in flavor. If you have a food processor, the grating of cheese is labor-free. I use a cylindrical hand grater (illustrated on p. 98) and have no problem whatsoever.

Similarly, fresh mushrooms should be used instead of canned ones. When possible in the summer, get farm fresh vegetables, or, even better, grow your own. The freshness and flavor of each of your ingredients will contribute to the over-all flavor of the finished pizza. You will find that it pays great dividends to spend a little extra time or money to procure ingredients that are bursting with fresh flavor.

TOMATO SAUCE FOR PIZZA

You can make this delicious sauce while the dough is rising. Making more than you will need for the pizza at hand is a good idea. The sauce keeps for quite a long time in the refrigerator and is handy for pasta, hot sandwiches, stews, and casseroles. You can also freeze some for your next pizza. Some people like to cook a sauce for several hours. If you choose to do this, you can probably eliminate the sugar, but the prolonged cooking will destroy some of the nutritional value of the sauce. I prefer to cook it for a short period of time and add just a little brown sugar. For about six cups of sauce.

¼ cup (4 tbsp.)	olive oil
2 cups	chopped onion
2 cloves	chopped garlic
5 cups (two 28 oz. cans)	Italian plum tomatoes, drained
1 tsp.	dried basil
1 tsp.	dried tarragon
2 tsp.	dried oregano
2 tsp.	salt
1 tbsp.	brown sugar
6 oz. (small can)	tomato paste
pepper	

Heat the oil in a heavy sauce pan. When the oil is hot, add the chopped onion and garlic and cook over medium heat until they are transparent. Add the tomatoes, chopping them up with your spoon in the pan. Rub the dried herbs between your hands and let them drop into the sauce. Add the salt, sugar, tomato paste and a few grindings of black pepper. Stir all of the ingredients together and simmer gently for 40 minutes, regulating the flame so that the sauce does not reach a boil.

If you like a smooth sauce, you may put it through a food mill or blend it in an electric blender after it has cooled. I like a pizza sauce that still has pieces of tomato in it. The pieces should not, however, be too large. It is easy to chop up the tomatoes as you stir the sauce.

PIZZA MARGHERITA

This is the pizza that Queen Margherita of Italy chose as her favorite among the pizzas presented to her by the chef Esposito in 1889. It has become a classic here in America. If you grow fresh basil or can get some in an Italian market or a farmers' market, chop it fine and use it in place of the dried basil. For two 12" thin-crust pizzas.

1 recipe	basic pizza dough (p. 14)
3-4 cups	tomato sauce for pizza (p. 27)
2-4 cups	sliced or grated mozzarella cheese
½ cup	grated parmesan or romano cheese
4 tbsp.	olive oil
2 tsp. or	dried basil
½ cup	chopped fresh basil

When the dough has risen for 1½ hours, preheat the oven to 500°. Divide the dough into 2 equal balls and roll them out on a floured board. Slip the dough onto a pizza pan, baking sheet, or baking stone that has been sprinkled with cornmeal. Roll up the edges to form a rim and brush the dough with olive oil. Spread the mozzarella cheese over the dough and then spoon the sauce over the cheese. Sprinkle 1 tsp. of dried basil on each of the pizzas by rubbing it between the palms of your hands and letting it fall on the sauce. Distribute the grated parmesan or romano cheese on top and then dribble olive oil over the whole thing. Bake for 10 to 15 minutes, until the crust is golden brown.

PIZZA CAPRICCIOSA

This pizza was a favorite among American soldiers in Rome during the second world war. The traditional fillings are given below, but you may substitute your favorite ingredients freely. For one 12" pizza.

½ recipe	basic pizza dough (p. 14)
1½ - 2 cups	tomato sauce for pizza (p. 27)
1 - 2 cups	grated mozzarella cheese
½ cup	freshly grated parmesan or romano cheese
2 tbsp.	olive oil
4 - 5	mushrooms, sliced
2 slices	prosciutto, cut into strips
12 mussels	shelled
1 egg	hard-boiled and peeled
4 strips	anchovy

When the dough has risen for 1½ hours, preheat the oven to 500°. Roll out the dough and turn up the edge to form a rim. Slip the dough onto a pizza pan, baking sheet or pizza stone that has been sprinkled with cornmeal. Brush the dough with olive oil and distribute the mozzarella cheese over it. Spread the sauce evenly over the cheese and then divide the pie into quarters by placing the strips of anchovy so that they radiate out from the center. Slice the hard-boiled egg into spears and place them in the center, also radiating out, like a star.

In one quadrant, distribute the sliced mushrooms; in the second, the prosciutto; in the third, the mussels; the fourth should be left plain. Sprinkle the top with the parmesan cheese and dribble the remaining olive oil over the whole thing. Bake for 10 to 15 minutes until the crust is golden brown.

PIZZA POMPEII

If you like garlic bread, you will like the kind of pizza that was made for hundreds of years before the introduction of the tomato into Italian cookery. This simple pizza was a poor man's repast; but, as you will see, it was a tasty and satisfying meal. The flour that was used by the Romans was probably coarser than the flour you will use, and their yeast was slower-acting. Yeast was kept alive, before it could be conveniently purchased in little pre-measured packages, by saving a piece of the dough each time bread was made and using it to grow the next batch of yeast. Neighbors would share the yeast and keep a culture alive for generations. Oil was not used in preparing the dough back in Roman days, so the crust was relatively hard and crisp. For one 12" pizza.

½ recipe	basic pizza dough, without the olive oil (p. 14)
¼ cup	olive oil
3 cloves	garlic, sliced paper thin
¼ cup	black or green olives sliced
1 tsp.	dried oregano
salt	

Make the pizza dough without adding any of the oil. Reserve the oil for later. When the dough has risen for 1½ hours, preheat the oven to its hottest temperature (500°, if possible). Roll the dough out into 1 large pizza or 2 smaller ones. Roll up the edge of the dough to form a rim and slide the dough onto a pizza pan, baking sheet or baking stone that has been sprinkled with cornmeal. Brush the dough liberally with olive oil and distribute the garlic and olives over the dough. Rub the oregano between the palms of your hands and let the crumbled bits fall evenly on the pizza. This will release the flavor of the herb. Sprinkle just a little salt on top and dribble the remaining oil on the dough. Bake for about 10 minutes until the crust is crisp and golden brown.

PIZZA NAPOLETANA

This is another classic pizza that you will find emerging from the famous brick ovens of Naples. For two 12" thin-crust pizzas.

1 recipe	basic pizza dough (p. 14)
3 - 4 cups	tomato sauce for pizza (p. 27)
4 tbsp.	olive oil
16 fillets	anchovy
2 - 3 cups	grated mozzarella cheese
1 - 2 cups	grated parmesan cheese
6 tbsp.	capers

After the dough has risen for 1½ hours, preheat the oven to 500°. Divide the dough into 2 equal balls and roll out each of them. Make a rim and slip the dough onto pizza pans that have been sprinkled with cornmeal. Brush the dough with half of the olive oil, a tbsp. for each pie. Distribute half of the tomato sauce over each, spreading the sauce with the back of a spoon. Put 8 anchovy fillets on each of the pizzas and sprinkle the capers liberally on each. Then distribute half of each kind of cheese over the top and dribble 1 tbsp. of olive oil on each. Bake for 10 to 15 minutes until the crust is golden brown.

PIZZA DI SCAMMERO

This savory pizza pocket is for anchovy lovers. If you enjoy the taste of braised chicory, but do not care for anchovies, try substituting tuna for a lighter fish flavor.

There is always confusion over terminology between endive and chicory in French, Italian and English. The kind of lettuce this recipe calls for is the curly-leaf lettuce commonly called chicory in supermarkets. You may think that two heads is too much, but it cooks way down. If you are fortunate enough to live in a place where Italian black olives are available, by all means use them instead of the bland American variety. For one semi-circular pizza pocket.

½ recipe	basic pizza dough (p. 14)
2 heads	chicory
6 tbsp.	olive oil
1 clove	garlic
2 tbsp.	capers
6 black olives	pitted and chopped
2 tbsp.	raisins
6 fillets	anchovy cut in small pieces or 1 small can tuna
¼ tsp.	salt
pepper	
1 egg yolk	

Prepare the chicory while the dough is rising. Set a large pot of water to boil on the stove. Chop the chicory into medium small pieces. When the water has reached a rolling boil, put all of the chicory into it as quickly as possible and then turn off the heat. Let the chicory blanch for 1 minute and then drain the water and dry off the leaves. Heat 4 tbsp. of the olive oil in a large frying pan and brown the clove of garlic in the oil. When the garlic is brown, remove it and throw it away. Put the chicory in the oil with the salt and some pepper. Stir the chicory in the hot oil for about 5 minutes. It will become slightly transparent and bright in color. Do not let it brown. Remove the pan from the heat while there is still some crunch left in the thickest pieces of lettuce. Set the chicory aside to cool.

When the dough has risen for 1½ hours, preheat the oven to 450°. Roll out the dough and slip it onto a baking sheet or pizza pan that has been sprinkled with cornmeal. Brush the dough with 1 tbsp. of olive oil. Spread the cooled chicory leaves over half of the dough, leaving a rim of at least 1 inch around the filled edge. Distribute the capers, chopped olives, anchovy pieces and raisins on the chicory.

Fold the unfilled half of the dough over the filling and roll the edges together to form a rim. Mix the remaining oil and the egg yolk together and brush the dough with this glaze. Bake for about 25 minutes or until the crust is golden brown and glistening.

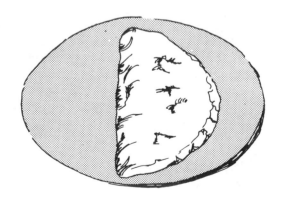

PESTO PIZZA

Pesto is a Genoese specialty that is becoming more and more popular in the United States. It is a blend of fresh basil, garlic, nuts and cheese that can **only** be made with fresh basil leaves in season. I know several people (I am one) who reserve a row in their summer gardens for the cultivation of basil in order to have pesto. Fortunately, the mixture can be frozen with great success and enjoyed throughout the year. Because only a few tablespoons of pesto are needed to season a whole pot of spaghetti or a whole pizza, a good supply can be stored conveniently without taking up too much room in your freezer. If you freeze it, leave out the parmesan cheese; add the cheese to the mixture after it is defrosted. Pesto is not cooked; it is simply warmed.

A pizza made with pesto is not very far from the original herb and garlic pizza. There is nothing in the pesto pizza that was not available to the Roman breakfaster. Many pesto recipes call for pine nuts, but I use walnuts.

PESTO

2 cups	chopped fresh basil leaves
1 cup	olive oil
2 tbsp.	chopped pine nuts or walnuts
¾ cup	grated parmesan cheese
½ tsp.	salt
3 cloves (or more)	garlic

The ingredients for pesto can be worked into a paste with a large mortar and pestle, but if you have a blender, you will find it much easier to prepare. Put all of the ingredients in the blender, except the parmesan cheese. Blend at high speed until they are thoroughly combined. Empty the blender into a bowl and add the grated parmesan cheese to the mixture. It should have the consistency of paste when all of the ingredients are mixed. You may store this mixture in the refrigerator for a number of weeks if it is well-covered. The top of the mixture may darken slightly, but stirring the mixture will restore the proper color. Pesto is delicious on hot cooked green beans or potatoes as well as on pasta.

For one thin-crust 12" pizza.

½ recipe	basic pizza dough (p. 14)
1 recipe	pesto

After the dough has risen for 1½ hours, preheat the oven to 500°. Roll out the dough and form a rim around the edge. Slip the dough onto a pizza pan, baking sheet, or baking stone that has been sprinkled with cornmeal. Brush the dough with olive oil and put an ovenproof plate or smaller baking tin in the middle of the dough so that the center will not rise or bubble as the crust bakes. Bake the unfilled dough in the oven for about 10 minutes or until it is golden. Remove the almost-baked crust and spread the pesto on it. Return it to the oven and cook for another 2 to 3 minutes. Remove when the crust is fully done. Do not let the pesto turn to dark green. It should really just be heated, not cooked.

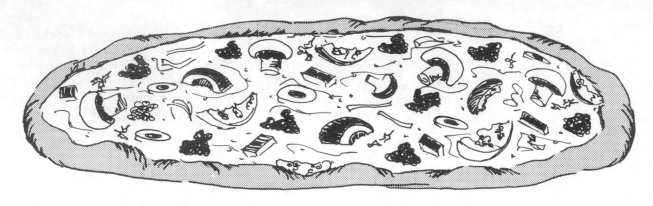

FESTIVE SAUSAGE PIZZA

This aromatic pizza is good for special occasions, especially when feasting is the form the celebration takes. You can make very small pizzas and serve them as tasty (but filling) hors d'oeuvres for a party. This recipe makes one 13" deep dish pizza.

1 recipe	basic pizza dough (p. 14)
3 tsp.	powdered cardamom
3 tbsp.	olive oil
1 cup	chopped onion
1 clove	chopped garlic
2 cups	drained Italian tomatoes
½ small can	tomato paste
1 tsp.	brown sugar
1 tsp.	salt
black pepper	
orange peel	
1 tsp.	fennel
½ tsp.	dried basil
½ tsp.	dried oregano
¼ tsp.	tarragon
1 lb.	sweet Italian sausage
2 cups (½ lb.)	grated mozzarella cheese
¾ cup	freshly grated parmesan or romano cheese

Make the dough according to the basic instructions, but add the cardamom after you add the yeast mixture. While the dough is rising, you can make the sauce. Cook the sausage either in a pan in the oven or on top of the stove. This will remove much of the fat. When the sausage is fully cooked, drain it on paper towels and slice it into small pieces.

In a separate saucepan, heat 2 tbsp. of the oil and cook the chopped onion and garlic over a medium heat until they are transparent. Add the tomatoes, tomato paste, salt, sugar, herbs, and orange peel, and simmer for 40 minutes. Chop up the large pieces of tomato with a spoon as you stir. When the sausage is cooked, drained, and cut up, you should add it to the sauce and let it simmer for the rest of the cooking time.

When the sauce is ready and the dough has risen for 1½ hours, preheat the oven to 450°. Roll out the dough and place it in the deep dish pizza pan. Press the dough onto the edges of the pan and neatly cut off any excess that hangs over the rim. Brush the dough with oil and spread the sauce with the sausage over the dough. Cover the sauce with the cheeses and dribble olive oil on the top. Bake for 25 minutes or until the crust is golden brown.

STUFFED PIZZA RUSTICA
WITH SPINACH

Stuffed pizza may be made with any filling you like, but this is my favorite. This recipe is for a stuffed, semi-circular pizza pocket. Stuffed pizza may also be made in the form of a pie with an upper crust and a bottom crust. To make this kind of stuffed pizza, simply put one layer of pizza dough in the bottom of a large pie pan or deep dish pizza pan, fill it with the ingredients of your choice and cover with the second crust. Crimp the edges together with your fingers and make three little slits in the top of the crust.

I prefer the semi-circular stuffed pizzas because they look elegant and because you can make two different kinds simultaneously. The glaze is optional but well worth the extra minute it takes.

This recipe will make two semi-circular (calzone-style) pizzas. The filling recipe is enough for both; however, you might want to make only half and try a different filling for the second pocket.

You may use any of the pizza doughs in Chapter II for making stuffed pizza, except the baking soda dough. It is fun to experiment with various flavors and colors in the dough and the filling.

1 recipe	basic pizza dough (p. 14)
1 lb.	ricotta cheese
2 cups	lightly steamed fresh spinach leaves
2 eggs	
1 tsp.	salt
black pepper	
nutmeg	
2 cups	grated mozzarella cheese
1½ lb.	sweet Italian sausage cooked, drained and sliced
or	
4 slices	prosciutto chopped
1 egg yolk	
1 tbsp.	olive oil

While the pizza dough is rising, you can make the stuffing. Put the ricotta cheese, spinach leaves, eggs and seasonings into the blender and blend at medium speed until they are well mixed. You may have to do this in several batches if your blender is not large. Cook the sausage in the oven or on top of the stove, drain off any extra fat and slice it into small pieces. Add the sausage (or prosciutto) and the mozzarella cheese to the spinach mixture.

When the dough has risen for 1½ hours, preheat the oven to 400°. Prepare the stuffed pizza according to the directions on page 16. Mix an egg yolk with 1 tbsp. of olive oil and brush it on the stuffed pockets with a pastry brush.

Bake for about 35 minutes or until the pizzas are golden brown.

DELI PIZZA

Use your favorite sandwich ingredients and your imagination. For one 12" thin-crust pizza.

½ recipe	rye pizza dough (p. 21)
2 tbsp.	olive oil
5 slices	Swiss cheese
2 large	dead ripe tomatoes
5 slices	baked ham
2 cups	grated mozzarella cheese
oregano	

When the dough has risen for 1½ hours, preheat the oven to 500°. Roll out the dough and make a rim around the edge. Slide the dough onto a pizza pan, baking sheet or baking stone that has been sprinkled with cornmeal. Brush the dough with 1 tbsp. of oil.

Lay the slices of Swiss cheese on the dough to cover the bottom of the pizza. Slice the tomatoes thin and shake some of the extra liquid out of them. Lay the tomato slices over the Swiss cheese. Now arrange the ham on top of the tomato slices. Cover the top with grated mozzarella and sprinkle with a little oregano and olive oil. Bake for 10 to 15 minutes until the crust is golden brown.

GARDENER'S NO-FLOUR PIZZA

This recipe does not include a bread dough, so it is not really a pizza. But it is a marvelous pizza-like dish for vegetarians and zuccini fanciers of all persuasions. It should be baked in a traditional pie pan, not a flat pizza pan. For a 9" pie pan.

3 cups	grated zuccini
2 eggs	beaten
2½ cups	grated mozzarella cheese
1½ cups	tomato sauce for pizza
1 small	green pepper, chopped
6 mushrooms	sliced
½ cup	parmesan cheese, grated
1 tsp.	dried oregano
1 tbsp.	olive oil

Heat the oven to 400°. Squeeze the excess moisture out of the grated zuccini with paper towels. Mix the zuccini, the 2 beaten eggs and 1½ cups of the mozzarella together and fill the bottom of the pie pan with the mixture. Bake the mixture for about 10 minutes. Remove the pan from the oven and spread the tomato sauce, the fresh vegetables and the remaining cheeses over the zuccini. Crumble the oregano between your hands onto the cheese. Dribble the olive oil over the top and bake for 25 minutes. Do not let the cheese get overly browned.

DOUBLE-CRUST SHRIMP PIZZA

The directions on pages 17-18 give complete details on how to assemble a double-crust pizza. This is the best method for preserving the moistness of delicate ingredients. For one double-crust pizza made in a 13" deep dish pizza pan.

1½ recipes	basic pizza dough (p. 14)
1½ - 2 cups	tomato sauce for pizza (p. 27)
2 tbsp.	olive oil
2 cups (½ lb.)	grated mozzarella cheese
¾ cup	freshly grated parmesan cheese
1 cup	finely chopped onion
1 green pepper	thinly sliced
1½ - 2 cups	cooked whole shrimp
oregano	
(capers)	

When the dough has risen for 1½ hours, preheat the oven to 500°. Roll out the bottom layer of the dough until it is larger than the deep dish pizza pan. Sprinkle the pan with cornmeal and place the dough in it, pressing the edges of the dough against the side of the pan. The dough should hang over the rim of the pan. Brush the dough with olive oil and sprinkle 1 cup of the grated mozzarella cheese over it. Distribute the shrimp, onions, green peppers, capers, and a little oregano over the dough. Place the second layer of dough over these ingredients and crimp the edges of the dough together around the rim of the pan. Carefully spread the sauce over the second layer and cover the sauce with the remaining cheeses. Crumble a little more oregano over the cheese and dribble the remaining tbsp. of olive oil over the top. Bake the about 25 minutes or until the crust is golden brown. Allow the pizza to cool for a few minutes before cutting.

FOUR CHEESE PIZZA

You may want to top this pizza with diced fresh tomatoes, chopped ham or crumbled pieces of crisp bacon. If you use the proportions of cheeses recommended below, the filling should have a slightly sharp cheese flavor. This will vary with the age and quality of the provolone you use. Try to get a real Italian provolone for the marvelous character it will lend to your pizza. You may vary the proportion of mozzarella to provolone to control the degree of sharpness. For one 12" thin-crust pizza.

½ recipe	basic pizza dough (p. 14)
6 oz.	ricotta cheese
¼ lb.	grated provolone
2 oz.	grated parmesan
½ lb.	grated mozzarella
2 eggs	lightly beaten
2 tbsp.	heavy cream
nutmeg	
2 tbsp.	freshly cut chives
1 tbsp.	olive oil

When the dough has risen for 1½ hours, preheat the oven to 450°. Roll the dough out and form a rim around the edge. Slip the dough onto a pizza pan, baking sheet or baking stone that has been sprinkled with cornmeal. Combine the provolone, parmesan, ricotta and ½ of the mozzarella with the beaten eggs, the cream, a dash of nutmeg and the chives in a bowl. Spread the cheese mixture evenly over the dough. Sprinkle with chopped tomatoes, ham, bacon, olives, or whatever you would like as an accenting flavor. Then distribute the rest of the mozzarella cheese over the top. Dribble the olive oil on the pizza and bake for about 20 minutes.

MEATBALL PIZZA

I like to make medium-sized meatballs and then cut them in half to place on this pizza. You may prefer to make tiny meatballs and put them on the pizza whole or great big meatballs and slice them. You will have to adjust your cooking time accordingly. If you make very large meatballs, they will have to be chilled before they can be sliced. For two 12" thin-crust pizzas.

1 recipe	basic pizza dough (p. 14)
1 recipe	tomato sauce for pizza
1 lb.	chopped round or other hamburger meat
¼ cup	freshly grated parmesan cheese
1 egg	beaten
1 slice	whole wheat bread
2 tbsp.	milk or cream
3 tbsp.	chopped fresh parsley
1 tsp.	salt
¼ tsp.	allspice, ground
2 cloves	garlic
⅓ cup	olive oil
1½ cup	grated mozzarella cheese

Make the meatballs while the dough is rising. Start right away because you will want them to chill for 1 hour before cooking them. The chilling time helps keep the meatballs in shape while they are cooking.

Put the slice of bread in the bottom of a large mixing bowl and soak it in the milk and the beaten egg until it becomes soft. Mash the bread up with a fork, then add the meat, parmesan cheese, parsley, salt, allspice, and the 2 cloves of garlic crushed in a garlic press. Mix the ingredients well and then form the meatballs by rolling pieces of the mixture between the palms of your hands. Try to make the balls as nearly round as possible and uniform in size. As you make each meatball, place it on a clean platter. When you have used up all of the meat mixture, cover the platter and place it in the refrigerator for an hour.

Heat 2 tbsp. of olive oil in a heavy frying pan. Cook as many meatballs at a time as you can without crowding them. Don't allow the meatballs to stick to the pan; keep rolling the balls around in the pan. If they should begin to stick, free them with a spatula. Medium-sized meatballs will take about 10 minutes to cook thoroughly. They will be browned on the outside and cooked through on the inside. Remove each batch of meatballs from the pan as they are done and cook another batch, until they are all done.

When the dough has risen for 1½ hours, preheat the oven to 450°. Divide the dough into 2 equal parts. Roll each part out and form a rim around the edge of each. Slip them onto pizza pans, baking sheets or baking stones that have been sprinkled with cornmeal. Brush the dough with olive oil and spread half of the tomato sauce on each pizza. Cut the meatballs in half and distribute them all over the pizzas, flat side down. Cover the pizzas with the grated mozzarella cheese, and dribble olive oil over each. Bake for about 20 minutes until the crusts are golden brown.

EGGPLANT PIZZA

Bean sprouts can be purchased in health food stores or grown at home. If you use sprouts other than mung or lentil, be sure that they are suitable for cooking. Alfalfa sprouts, for example, can be sprinkled on the pizza after it is cooked but will not fare well in the oven.

Tofu is a high-protein soybean product that has the appearance of a white custard cut into blocks. It has a bland flavor that mixes well with other ingredients. It can be obtained in Japanese food stores, health food stores, and in cans in some supermarkets. Fresh tofu is always preferable. For one thin-crust 12" pizza.

½ recipe	whole wheat dough (p. 20)
1½ cups	tomato sauce for pizza (p. 27)
1 large	eggplant
6 tbsp.	olive oil
1 tsp.	dried basil
1 tbsp.	lemon juice
¾ cup	mung bean sprouts
¾ cup	lentil sprouts
¼ lb.	tofu diced into small cubes
2 - 3 tbsp.	sesame seeds
1½ cups	mozzarella cheese, grated
½ cup	parmesan cheese, grated
salt	

While the dough is rising, prepare the eggplant. Slice the eggplant into ½ inch slices, sprinkle salt on both sides and place between paper towels for a half hour to remove excess liquid. Heat the oven to 400°. In a small bowl, mix 4 tbsp. of the olive oil with the lemon juice and crumble the basil into the mixture by rubbing it between the palms of your hands. Pat the eggplant slices dry and brush the olive oil mixture onto both sides. Lay the slices in a baking pan (preferably glass) and bake in the oven for 10 to 15 minutes. Remove them from the baking sheet immediately. They may be piled up on a plate until you are ready to use them.

When the dough has risen for 1½ hours, set the oven at 450°. Roll the dough out and form a rim around the edge. Slide the dough onto a pizza pan, baking sheet or baking stone that has been sprinkled with cornmeal. Brush the dough with 1 tbsp. of olive oil and spread the sauce evenly over it.

Make a layer of eggplant slices on top of the sauce. Sprinkle the bean sprouts, tofu and sesame seeds over the eggplant. Then distribute the grated cheeses over the top and dribble the remaining olive oil onto the cheese. Bake for about 15 minutes. The crust should be hard to the touch; the cheese should be melted and just beginning to brown. Do not let the cheese brown too much.

HAWAIIAN SWEET AND SOUR PIZZA

You can judge the ripeness of a pineapple, I have discovered, by looking at the bottom part of the fruit. If the bumps near the bottom are separated and the space between them is yellow, the pineapple is ripe. Cut the pineapple into cubes by first carving it into thick slices (about ½"). Then remove the skin and the fibrous inner core from each slice so you have rings of pineapple flesh. Cut these rings into ½" cubes. For two 12" thin-crust pizzas.

1 recipe	basic pizza dough (p. 14)
3 - 4 cups	tomato sauce for pizza (p. 27)
1 lb.	slab of cooked ham
or	
1 lb.	cooked shrimp, peeled and deveined
1 pineapple	cut into ½" cubes
2 green peppers	coarsely chopped
½ lb.	gruyere cheese, sliced thin
½ cup	freshly grated parmesan
2 tbsp.	olive oil

When the dough has risen for 1½ hours, preheat the oven to 450°. Divide the dough in half and roll out each piece until it is slightly larger than the pan. Slip the dough onto pizza pans, baking sheets or pizza stones which have been sprinkled with cornmeal. Roll up the edges to form rims. Brush with olive oil. Spread the sauce over the pizzas and distribute the chunks of ham (or shrimp), pineapple and pieces of green pepper over the sauce. Arrange the slices of gruyere and the grated parmesan over the top of each. Bake at 450° for 15 to 20 minutes, until the crusts are golden brown.

MEXICAN PIZZA

This recipe creates a pizza that may be too hot for the average palate, so be sure to vary the "hot" ingredients to suit your taste. For one 13" deep dish pizza.

1 recipe	basic pizza dough (p. 14)
1 lb.	ground beef
1 lb.	grated monterey jack cheese
1 lb.	grated cheddar or colby cheese
1 can (6 oz.)	jalapeno peppers
1 package	taco seasoning
1½ cups	Mexican salsa (tomato and chili sauce)
3 tbsp.	olive oil

While the dough is rising (1½ hours), brown the ground beef and taco seasoning together. Drain. Preheat the oven to 450° when you are ready to roll out the dough. Roll out the dough to form a circle slightly larger than the pizza pan and place the dough in the pan. Press the dough to the sides of the pan and cut off any excess dough that hangs over the rim. Brush the dough with olive oil.

Combine the cheeses and spread two-thirds of the mixture over the dough. Distribute the jalapeno peppers over the cheese and then spread the ground beef over the peppers. Next, spread the salsa as evenly as possible over the entire pizza and sprinkle the remaining cheese over the sauce. Dribble olive oil over the top and bake for 25 minutes or until the crust is golden brown.

LOW CALORIE PIZZA

Pizza does not have to be a fattening dish. The more oil and other fats you eliminate from the dough and the filling, the less fat you will have to worry about. Mozzarella is a relatively low calorie cheese, and many of the best pizza fillings are diet foods anyway. Of course, the pizza isn't quite as yummy with the olive oil taken out, but you have the satisfaction of knowing that it is no more fattening than a fresh vegetable sandwich. You may want to serve fresh lemon slices and a little freshly grated parmesan cheese on the side. If you are dieting, don't eat the whole pizza by yourself. Invite your friends over and just eat one slice each. For one 12" thin crust pizza.

½ recipe	basic pizza dough, without the olive oil (p. 14)
2 tomatoes	chopped and drained
1 onion	thinly sliced
1 green pepper	thinly sliced
6 or more	fresh mushrooms, sliced
¾ cup	grated mozzarella cheese
oregano	
salt and pepper	
garlic powder	

Don't forget to leave the olive oil out of the dough. When the dough has risen for 1½ hours, preheat the oven to 450°. Roll out the dough and form a rim around the edge. Slide it onto a pizza pan, baking sheet or baking stone that has been sprinkled with cornmeal. Distribute the fresh vegetables on the dough and crumble the oregano over them. Sprinkle salt, pepper, and garlic powder sparingly over the ingredients. Cover the vegetables with a light layer of grated mozzarella cheese. Bake for 15 to 20 minutes until the crust is golden brown.

PIZZA FRUTTI DI MARE

You can add or substitute your favorite "fruit of the sea" for the seafood given here. Scallops, mussels, clams, anchovies--even sardines! For two 12" thin-crust pizzas.

1 recipe	basic pizza dough (p. 14)
3 - 4 cups	tomato sauce for pizza (p. 27)
4 tbsp. (¼ cup)	olive oil
1 can (7 oz.)	tuna fish, drained of all liquid
½ lb.	shrimp, cooked, peeled and deveined
½ cup	sliced green olives
½ cup	sliced black olives
½ cup	capers
2 - 3 cups	grated mozzarella cheese
1 cup	grated parmesan or romano cheese

After the dough has risen for 1½ hours, preheat the oven to 450°. Divide the dough into equal parts and roll each part out. Slide the dough onto pizza pans, baking sheets, or baking stones and roll up the edge to form a rim. Brush each with a tbsp. of olive oil and cover with tomato sauce. Distribute the tuna fish, olives and capers over both of the pizzas. Cut the shrimp in half the long way and divide them between the 2 pizzas. Sprinkle the mozzarella and parmesan cheeses over the top and dribble the remaining olive oil over them. Bake for 15 to 20 minutes, until the crust is golden brown.

DEEP DISH CHILI PIZZA

This is a mild chili for the American taste. You can increase the spiciness of the chili by using more chili powder or by adding dried, red-hot peppers. If some of your pizza-eaters like their chili hot and others like it mild, you can serve a hot Mexican salsa on the side. This pizza should be served with a variety of garnishes, such as chopped sweet onion, chopped fresh tomatoes, sour cream, green pepper, or guacamole (see recipe on p. 60). You may also want to put slices of avocado on the chili before covering it with the cheese for a delicious variation on the basic recipe. For one 14" deep dish pizza.

1 recipe	basic pizza dough (p. 14)
2 tbsp.	olive oil
1 large	onion
1 clove	garlic, minced
1 lb.	hamburger meat
1 large can (28 oz.)	Italian plum tomatoes
2 cans (15 oz. each)	red kidney beans
1 tbsp.	chili powder
1 tsp.	ground cumin
1 tsp.	salt
1 bayleaf	
¼ oz.	unsweetened baker's chocolate
2 cups	grated cheddar cheese

You can make the chili while the dough is rising. Heat the oil in a large frying pan and cook the chopped onions and garlic in it over medium heat for 6 or 7 minutes until they are transparent. Add the hamburger meat and brown it with the onions. If the meat gives up a lot of fat, tip the pan and spoon it out. Drain as much liquid as you can out of the tomatoes and the kidney beans. Add them to the meat and onion mixture with the spices and the unsweetened chocolate. Cook over low flame for 1 hour. This chili has less liquid than usual, so you have to keep an eye on it to be sure that it does not burn. Mash some of the kidney beans with your spoon when you stir the chili. Most of the liquid will have cooked off by the time the chili is finished.

When the dough has risen for 1½ hours, preheat the oven to 450°. Roll out the dough so that it is larger than the pan. Slip the dough over the deep dish pan that has been sprinkled with cornmeal. Press the dough against the edges of the pan and neatly trim the overhanging dough. Brush with olive oil. Then spread the chili over the dough and cover with grated cheddar cheese. Bake for about 20 minutes, until the crust is golden brown.

PIZZA FLORENTINE
(ARTICHOKE PIZZA)

My thanks to Mary Nell Reck of LaCuisine in Houston for letting me reprint her recipe here. For one 12" thin-crust pizza.

½ recipe	basic pizza dough (p. 14)
3 tbsp.	olive oil
2 cloves	garlic, chopped
2 - 3 tbsp.	onion, finely chopped
3 large ripe	tomatoes, peeled, juice removed and finely chopped
or	
1 large can (28 oz.)	Italian plum tomatoes, drained
1 tsp.	oregano
1 can	artichoke hearts, packed in water, sliced
1 cup	grated mozzarella cheese
6 tbsp.	freshly grated parmesan cheese
salt	
pepper	

Heat the olive oil in a saute pan. Stir in the garlic and onions. Saute over moderate heat for about 4 minutes. Stir in the tomatoes which have been skinned, drained of juice and chopped. Cook, stirring occasionally, until the sauce is thick and pasty. Season with salt and freshly ground black pepper to taste.

When the dough has risen for 1½ hours, preheat the oven to 450°. Roll out the dough and slip it onto a baking sheet, pizza pan, or pizza stone. Roll up the edge to form a rim. Spread the prepared sauce over the pizza dough and sprinkle with the mozzarella cheese. Cover with the sliced and broken up pieces of artichoke hearts. Lightly sprinkle oregano over everything and bake for 20 to 30 minutes. Remove from the oven. Sprinkle with the parmesan cheese. Serve immediately.

SKILLET PIZZA

You can make pizza in a frying pan on top of the stove. This technique should only be used, however, when an oven is not available. The skillet method will not give you as beautiful a crust as the usual oven-method. However, a time may come in each of our lives when we want to make a homemade pizza and have no access to an oven. When that time comes, make skillet pizza!

The trick is to keep the flame low enough so the dough doesn't burn on the bottom. The crust will brown on the side that touches the pan, but will not get brown on the other side. You could conceivably make this pizza over a camp fire if you can keep the heat low enough, but I must admit I have never tried it.

You may adjust the proportion of ingredients to match the size of your skillet. I make mine in a 10-incher.

¼ recipe	basic pizza dough (p. 14)
¼ cup	olive oil or other vegetable oil
1 cup	tomato sauce for pizza (p. 27)
1 tsp.	dried oregano
4 oz.	grated mozzarella cheese
3 tbsp.	freshly grated parmesan cheese

After the dough has risen for 1½ hours, roll it out until it is slightly larger than your skillet. Put 3 tbsp. of oil in the skillet and roll it around until the entire inside surface is well coated. Lift the dough onto the skillet and fit the dough against the sides. Take a rolling pin and roll it over the top edge of the skillet to remove the extra dough that is hanging down. Brush the inside of the dough with the remaining tbsp. of oil.

Spread the pizza sauce over the bottom and distribute the mozzarella cheese. Crumble the oregano between your hands and let it fall over the cheese. Put a cover on the skillet and cook over low heat for 20 minutes. Check regularly to be sure that the dough is not burning. You can do this by lifting the edge of the pizza carefully away from the side of the pan and peeking down to the bottom. After 20 minutes, sprinkle the freshly grated parmesan cheese over the pizza. Replace the cover and cook for another 5 to 10 minutes. When the pizza is done, you will be able to slide it out of the skillet onto a platter for cutting.

IV

THE MORNING AFTER

Special Pizzas for Sunday Brunch

Pizza, which started in Roman times as a breakfast food, makes a marvelous brunch menu. Most of the recipes in this book can be adapted for brunch, especially if you make them in smaller, individual sizes.

The recipes in this chapter were chosen especially for brunch dishes because they are festive, fun-to-eat, and a little out of the ordinary. If your gatherings are informal, you might let your guests help you roll out the dough. Make your brunch a participatory project and share the responsibility for the results.

If you have a big kitchen and adventurous friends, try a "pizza bar" where the guests create their own favorite pizzas. All you have to do is make a big batch of dough in advance and have the garnishes chopped and ready. Cut up onions, mushrooms, green pepper, pepperoni, tomatoes, olives, and bacon bits. Have grated mozzarella and parmesan cheeses ready in bowls and be sure to have a variety of dried herbs on hand and some garlic salt. Let the guests roll out their own dough and place it in a tart tin or foil tin from frozen pot pies. The guests create their own pizzas.

You can avoid being left alone in the kitchen during your party if you bring the party in there with you!

ANTIPASTO PIZZETTE

Choose your favorite antipasto fixings and feature them on little pizzas. The combination below tastes great for starters. Serve the pizzette with lemon wedges and a bowl of freshly grated parmesan cheese on the side. For six little pizzas.

1 recipe	basic pizza dough (p. 14)
1 clove	garlic
¾ cup	olive oil
2 onions	sliced
2 tomatoes	chopped
1 green pepper	sliced
2 eggs	hard boiled and chopped
4 tbsp.	capers
½ cup	sliced green olives
½ cup	sliced black olives
1 cup	roasted sweet red pepper cut in strips
12 pepperoncini	(pickled Italian peppers)
1 can	tuna fish
2 cups (½ lb.)	grated mozzarella cheese
1 cup	grated parmesan cheese
oregano	
lemon wedges	
salt and pepper	

Put the olive oil in a heavy skillet and brown the peeled clove of garlic. Remove the garlic and save the oil. When the dough has risen for 1½ hours, preheat the oven to 500°. Divide the dough into 6 equal parts and roll each of them out to make a 6" pizza. Place them on baking sheets or baking tiles that have been sprinkled with cornmeal.

Brush each of the pizzas with the garlic-flavored olive oil. Distribute the antipasto ingredients evenly on the 6 pizzas (onions, tomatoes, peppers, eggs, capers, olives, pepperoncini, tuna). Put the grated mozzarella cheese over the antipasto ingredients; it will help protect them from drying out in the oven. Dribble olive oil on each and crumble the oregano between the palms of your hands over them. A very small amount of salt and pepper may be dashed over the pizzette, but for most tastes they will be salty enough without it. Bake for 10 minutes.

DEEP-FRIED HAM AND CHEESE CALZONE

These are so good you can have them for breakfast, lunch, dinner, brunch, or midnight snacks. They are even good cold, in a lunch box. The ham and cheese combination is our favorite, but try sausage, spinach, tomatoes, eggs, vegetables--whatever strikes your fancy. Also try different kinds of dough to create different flavors.

See Chapter II page 18 for directions on how to cut out and stuff the dough. For 25 small calzone.

1 recipe	basic pizza dough (p. 14)
1 cup (¼ lb.)	grated mozzarella cheese
¼ cup	grated parmesan cheese
3 slices	ham or prosciutto chopped up
cooking oil for deep frying	

In a bowl, mix the cheeses and chopped ham. Start heating the oil as you cut out the dough. In the center of each 4" circle of dough, put a tbsp. of the cheese and ham mixture. Moisten the edge of the dough and seal the calzone into little stuffed pockets. Deep fry according to instructions on page 18.

BLEU CHEESE PIZZA

Some recipes are naturals for making in miniature. This one is wonderful for tiny hors d'oeuvres as well as for individual pizzas. For six individual pizzas.

1 recipe	basic pizza dough (p. 14)
¾ lb.	bleu cheese
2 green peppers	chopped
6 scallions	chopped
2 tomatoes	chopped and drained
(3 tbsp.	sliced green olives)
3 tbsp.	chopped fresh parsley
3 tbsp.	freshly grated parmesan or romano cheese

When the dough has risen for 1½ hours, preheat the oven to 450°. Divide the dough into 6 parts and roll each out on a floured board. Roll up the edges of the dough to form rims and slide the shells onto baking sheets, pizza pans, or baking tiles that have been sprinkled with cornmeal.

Crumble the bleu cheese in a bowl, breaking up any large chunks. Distribute the chopped green pepper, scallion, and tomato (and green olives, if you like) among the pizzas and sprinkle the bleu cheese over the top. Bake for 15 to 20 minutes, until the crust is golden brown and the cheese is melted.

When you remove the pizzas from the oven, sprinkle the top with a little chopped fresh parsley and freshly grated parmesan cheese.

WRAPPED CAMEMBERT

Delight your friends with this rich and elegant dish. Serve it as an accompaniment to a big salad or a light vegetarian dish. You may use brie in place of the camembert, if you prefer. Serves four.

½ recipe	brioche pizza dough (p. 23)
½ lb.	camembert or brie cheese
1 egg	
1 tsp.	vegetable oil or melted butter

When the dough has risen for 2 hours, roll it out into a 12" circle. Cut the edges off the cheese and place it in the middle of the dough. Gather the dough neatly around the cheese and seal the seams by pinching the dough together. Be sure that all the seams are well sealed so the cheese does not leak out as it begins to melt inside the dough.

Turn the dough over onto a buttered baking sheet or pizza pan. Drape it with a clean dish towel and let it sit for 2 hours in a warm, draft-free place. Preheat the oven to 450°. Let it preheat fully before putting in the dough.

Beat the egg yolk with 1 tsp. vegetable oil or melted butter, and brush the glaze onto the dough. Bake for 5 minutes at 450°, then lower the heat to 375° and bake for 12 to 15 minutes longer. Slice the bread into quarters and serve.

SHIRRED EGG PIZZA

This isn't really a pizza at all. I have tried and tried to make this dish with bread dough but without proper results. So, here is a wonderful cheese pastry dough called gougere (see Chapter V). It is such a wonderful brunch dish that I just had to include it. If you have small tartlet tins, here's a chance to use them. They give an attractive, fluted look to the crust after it is cooked and removed from the tin. If you don't have tartlet tins, frozen pot pie tins will produce excellent results. To serve six.

Gougere

1¼ cup	water
1 cup (8 tbsp.)	unsalted butter
½ tsp.	salt
pepper	
1¼ cup	unbleached all-purpose flour
5 eggs	
2 cups	grated Swiss cheese

Preheat the oven to 400°. Use 1 tbsp. of butter to thoroughly grease the inside of the tins. Put the water, butter, salt and a little pepper in a pot and bring the water to a boil. Pour in all of the flour at once and stir until the ingredients are well mixed. Put the dough in a bowl and let it cool for a few minutes, stirring all the while. Add the eggs separately, stirring each into the mixture before you add the next. Then stir in the grated Swiss cheese. When all of the ingredients are thoroughly combined, line each of the tart tins with the dough. Use a spoon or your fingers to spread it evenly. Don't make the dough lining too thick. It will puff up a little as it cooks and you have to leave room for the filling. Bake for 20 minutes, then remove and add the filling. Don't open the oven during this initial baking period. Turn the heat down to 350° after you remove the shells.

Filling

6 slices	baked ham
1 large tomato	chopped and drained
1 cup	grated Swiss cheese
6 eggs	
salt	
pepper	
3 tbsp.	chopped parsley

Chop the ham into little pieces and divide it into 2 equal parts. Take 1 batch of the chopped ham and distribute it among the 6 shells. Then put a little of the chopped tomato in each. Break an egg into each shell and top with the remaining ham and the grated Swiss cheese. Be sure that the egg yolk is covered with cheese; this will protect it in the oven. Sprinkle a little salt and pepper on each and put the tarts back in the oven. In 12 minutes the dough will be finished and the egg will be soft-cooked. If you like an almost hard yolk, leave them in the oven for another 3 minutes.

When you take the shells out of the oven, remove them gently from the tins. Sprinkle the top of each with a little chopped fresh parsley and serve.

PIZZA EGG ROLLS

Like deep-fried calzone, pizza egg rolls may be made with any filling you like. These pizza egg rolls will be approximately the size of Chinese egg rolls. For 24 pizza egg rolls.

1 pkg. (1½ lbs.)	egg roll wrappers
2 lb.	mild Italian sausage
1 lb.	mozzarella cheese, grated
¼ lb.	parmesan or romano cheese, grated
2 tsp.	dried oregano
1 tsp.	garlic salt
1 cup (8 oz. can)	pizza sauce
1 egg	
cooking oil for deep frying	

If the egg roll wrappers are frozen, defrost them. Keep them wrapped so they will not dry out and become brittle. Cook the sausage in the oven or on top of the stove. Drain it and chop it into small pieces. Put 1½" of oil in a heavy saucepan or frying pan. Heat the oil slowly while you are preparing the filling. Put a piece of the dough into the oil so you will know when it is hot enough to begin cooking. The dough will begin to turn golden brown and puff up a little when the oil is sufficiently hot.

Combine the cooked sausage, grated cheeses, pizza sauce and seasonings in a large bowl. In another bowl beat the egg with some water. Take 1 egg roll wrapper at a time (keep the others covered so they don't dry out), and place a heaping tablespoon of filling in the middle of the wrapper. Fold 1 side over the filling and brush it with the egg mixture. Fold the other side over the first (the egg should seal the dough together). Brush more egg on the side that is facing up and fold the ends toward the middle. Press the pizza egg roll gently to seal it.

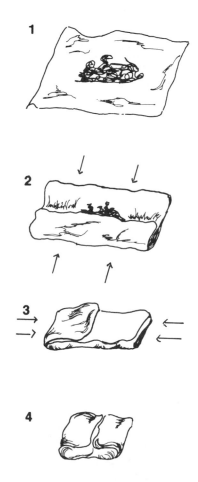

When the oil is hot, put as many of the pizza egg rolls in at a time as will fit without crowding. Fry for 10 minutes, turning each roll once with tongs. They should be crisp, puffy and golden brown. When you take the rolls out of the oil, drain them on paper towels to remove excess oil. Allow the pizza egg rolls to cool slightly before biting into them.

APPLE AND CHEDDAR CHEESE PIZZA

This is a beautiful-looking dish for brunch, as a side dish with pork or ham, or as a not-too-sweet dessert. If you wish to deemphasize its dessert-like qualities, make it with a whole wheat or rye crust instead of the brioche crust in this recipe. For one 12" pizza.

1 recipe	brioche dough (p. 23)
2 cups	applesauce
1½ tbsp.	cornstarch
3 tbsp.	light brown sugar
cinnamon	
6 apples	
¼ cup	butter
¼ cup	apricot jam
¼ - ½ lb.	cheddar cheese cut into julienne pieces
2 tbsp.	vegetable oil
1 egg yolk	

When the dough has risen for 2 hours, preheat the oven to 400°. Roll out the dough and slip it onto a pizza pan, baking sheet, or baking stone that has been sprinkled with cornmeal. Brush the dough with 1 tbsp. of oil. Put the applesauce in a bowl and stir in the sugar, cornstarch and a dash of cinnamon. Do not peel the apples, but slice them into thin, D-shaped slices. Spread the applesauce mixture over the dough and then arrange the apple slices on top. Begin in the middle of the pizza, and form a spiral of the apple slices, covering as much of the applesauce as you can.

Melt the butter in a small pan with the apricot jam. Use this mixture as a glaze for the apples. Brush the glaze on the apples quickly so they do not have a chance to discolor from prolonged contact with the air. Distribute the julienne slices of cheese on top of the apple slices, making them radiate out from the center like a starburst.

Mix the remaining tbsp. of oil with the egg yolk and brush the mixture onto the crust that is still exposed. Bake in the oven for about 20 minutes or until the crust is golden brown. After 15 minutes check the pizza regularly to be sure the crust is not getting overdone.

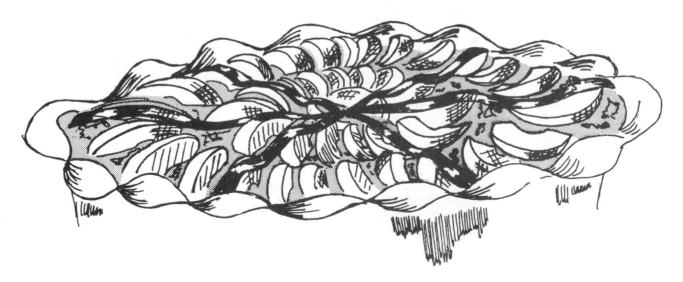

PIZZA SMORGASBORD

Make a variety of pre-cooked miniature pizza shells (pumpernickel, whole wheat, buttermilk) and set them out as you would bagels or rolls to make a do-it-yourself sandwichboard. The pizza shells appeal particularly to people who don't want the calories or carbohydrates of a two-slice sandwich. The little pizza rim keeps the ingredients from landing on the floor or on the laps of your guests.

You may use any of the recipes in Chapter II to make individual pre-cooked pizza shells. The recipes which call for four to five cups of flour will make about 15 bagel-size pizzas.

After the dough has risen for 90 minutes, flour a board and pull off a handful of dough at a time. Roll out each piece separately and turn up a little rim as you would for a large pizza.

Place the little shells on a baking sheet, pizza pan, or baking stone that has been sprinkled with cornmeal. When all the pizza shells are ready, put a piece of waxed paper on the bottom of each and place some weights on it (dry beans, rice, sterilized stones) so the crusts will not bulge up when baking. Brush the rims lightly with oil and bake at 400° for 15 to 20 minutes. Remove the weights after the first 10 minutes so the bottoms will brown. Remove the shells from the oven when they are nicely browned. Allow them to cool. Store in a plastic bag until you are ready to use them.

Below are some suggestions for fillings to set out for your smorgasbord.

creamed herring with onions
sliced tomatoes
sliced hard boiled eggs
smoked salmon
thinly sliced bermuda onion
thinly sliced Swiss or gruyere cheese
cream cheese
black olives chopped and mixed with
  mayonnaise
sliced cucumbers
liver pate
sliced pickles
thinly sliced ham or smoked sausage

ELEGANT SEAFOOD PIZZA

Why shouldn't pizza be elegant? The recipe below will give you pizzas that would be at home in Buckingham Palace. To achieve the full effect, take the time to boil the shrimp at home. Frozen pre-cooked shrimp will not pull their weight in this delicate combination of flavors. For six 6" pizzas.

1 recipe	basic pizza dough (p. 14)
½ lb.	scallops
½ lb.	fresh shrimp
½ lb.	fresh mushrooms
4 tbsp.	chopped shallots
1 tbsp.	brandy
½ cup (¼ lb.)	unsalted butter
4 tbsp.	olive oil or vegetable oil
4 tbsp.	flour
1 cup	clam broth
½ cup	whipping cream
½ lb.	gruyere cheese thinly sliced
1 cup	freshly grated parmesan cheese
½ cup	chopped fresh parsley
salt	
pepper	

For the shrimp boil

½	lemon
1	bay leaf
1	clove garlic
1 tsp.	whole allspice

While the dough is rising, prepare the filling. Slice the scallops very thin and pour the brandy over them with a little salt and pepper. Cover them and let them sit in the refrigerator for at least an hour.

Boil the water in a small pot with the bay leaf, peeled garlic, lemon, and allspice. When the water is boiling rapidly, put the shrimp in it and immediately turn off the heat. Let the shrimp sit in the hot water for 10 minutes until they are cooked through. Rinse the shrimp in cold water and peel and devein them. Slice in half the long way and set aside.

Wipe the mushrooms clean with a slightly damp cloth or mushroom brush and slice them very thin. Heat 4 tbsp. of butter with 2 tbsp. of oil in a saute pan. First cook the shallots over medium high heat for 5 minutes and then add the mushrooms. Saute the mushrooms for 4 minutes and then remove them to a plate. Add the marinated scallops to the saute pan and cook them for 5 minutes. Most of the butter and oil will be absorbed. Remove the scallops to the plate with the mushrooms.

Put another 4 tbsp. of butter in the pan and melt it. Add 4 tbsp. of flour to the butter and stir it in with a wire whisk. Cook the roux over low heat for 4 minutes, stirring constantly. Add the clam broth to which you have added any juice that ran off the mushrooms and scallops. Stir the liquid into the roux until it thickens. Then add the heavy cream and stir it constantly for 3 or 4 minutes. Add 6 slices of gruyere to the cream sauce. Allow the cheese to melt. This will make the sauce nice and thick and keep the pizza crust from getting soggy. Add the mushrooms, shrimp, and scallops to the sauce.

When the dough has risen for 1½ hours, preheat the oven to 450°. Divide the dough in 6 equal parts and roll each out to form 6" pizza crusts. Brush each with oil and then spread the seafood mixture over the dough. Top each pizza with slices of gruyere and grated parmesan cheese. Bake for about 15 minutes, until the crust is golden brown. After you remove the pizzas from the oven, sprinkle chopped fresh parsley over the top and serve.

VEGETARIAN WEDGE
(Four-Foot Pizza Hero)

You may wonder why this is called a "wedge" when it is one of the few dishes in this book that is not actually served in wedges. I checked into the matter and learned that the word "wedge" derives from the Old English word "wecg" (pronounced "wedge") which means, or meant, "lump." This wedge, however, is neither a wedge nor a lump. But it is a delicious brunch or lunch. It can be a little messy to eat; serve it only for the blue jean brunch bunch. If your guests are due to arrive in silk and linen, offer them something less hazardous to eat.

The wedge is only limited in size by the diagonal measurement of your oven. The biggest I can make is two feet. For two 2-foot wedges that will serve four to six people.

1 loaf (4 feet)	French bread
1 lb.	mozzarella cheese
1 cup	pizza sauce
4 mushrooms	sliced thin
1 green pepper	sliced thin
½ onion	sliced thin
6 tbsp.	olive oil
1 clove	garlic
½ tbsp.	vinegar
½ tsp.	tarragon
1 tsp.	oregano
½ tsp.	garlic salt

Line 2 shelves of the oven with aluminum foil and heat to 400°. Cut the bread into two, 2-foot pieces and slice each of them in half the long way. Remove as much of the soft inside of the bread as you can.

Heat the peeled clove of garlic in olive oil. When the garlic has browned, remove it and add the oregano, tarragon and vinegar to the oil. Mix them together thoroughly and brush onto the bread. Put the pieces of bread in the oven for 4 minutes.

Remove the bread and spread 2 tbsp. of sauce on each piece. On 2 of the pieces distribute the thinly sliced vegetables. Then cover all 4 pieces with mozzarella cheese. Put them back in the oven. After 5 minutes, brush them with the olive oil mixture and sprinkle a little garlic salt on each slice.

Cook for another 7 or 8 minutes until the mozzarella is melted, but not running out of the sandwich. Remove from the oven and put the unfilled halves on top of the filled halves. Serve piping hot.

V
VARIATIONS ON A NEOPOLITAN THEME

Analogies to Pizza From Around the World

When you're on to a good thing, everybody wants a piece of the pie. And everybody, sooner or later, comes up with the idea of cooking things in the oven on dough and melting cheese on top. If you look around in the world of international cookery, you will find a host of recipes that are really nothing more than thinly-disguised pizza. Every country may choose to include its own regional variety of dough and its local favorites as garnishes, but when you come right down to it, the idea is still the same. After all, bread and cheese are basics.

There are stuffed breads, hot open-face sandwiches, savory tarts, and phyllo pies, not to mention dumplings, crepes and pasties. The recipes in this chapter are just a sampling of the many dishes that are based on the same premise as pizza. Most of the recipes are made with bread dough, and all but one are cooked in the oven. Each constitutes a variation with its own unique flavor and character but also bears witness to the universality of the pizza-idea.

If you are a pizza lover already, you can't go wrong with these recipes. Give another country a chance to show what it can do with a little dough.

KASESCHNITTEN MIT CHAMPIGNONS
Switzerland

(Baked Cheese and Mushroom Sandwiches)

For six servings.

1 long loaf	French bread
¼ lb.	butter
1 tbsp.	vegetable oil
½ lb.	fresh mushrooms
½ cup	chopped scallions
3 tbsp.	flour
1 cup	half and half
½ - 1 cup	milk
salt	
pepper	
6 large slices	Swiss cheese
(6 eggs)	

Cut the French bread to make 6 long slices that fit your baking dish. They should be about 9" to 10" long and ½" thick. Melt 2 tbsp. of butter in a large frying pan and saute the bread slices on both sides. Add more butter if necessary. Place the fried bread slices in the baking pan.

In the same frying pan, melt another tbsp. of butter and add the tbsp. of vegetable oil. Wipe the mushrooms clean with a damp cloth and slice them. Saute the dry mushroom slices in the butter and oil for 5 minutes, then turn off the heat and stir in the chopped scallions, ½ tsp. salt and some freshly ground black pepper. Set the mushrooms aside.

Melt 4 tbsp. of butter in a saucepan. Add the flour to the butter slowly over low heat, stirring with a wire whisk. When all the butter has been incorporated into the flour to make a pasty roux, stop adding flour and continue to cook over low heat, stirring constantly for about 5 minutes. Still stirring, add the half and half. As the sauce warms, it will thicken. Continue to add milk to the sauce a little at a time. Let it thicken each time before you add more. When the sauce has reached the consistency of a thick cream sauce, stop adding milk. Add the mushroom and scallion mixture to the cream sauce. Taste the sauce for seasoning and add more salt and pepper if needed.

Preheat the oven to 350°. Spread the sauce and mushrooms over the bread slices in the baking pan and top each piece of bread with a slice of Swiss cheese.

Bake for 10 minutes, until the cheese melts over the mushroom sauce. For a variation, while the sandwiches are baking, fry or poach 6 eggs and place them on top of the sandwiches when they come out of the oven.

BURAG B'JEBEN
India

(Cheese Wrapped in Dough)

For about 16 burags.

1½ cups	crumbled feta cheese
½ cup	cottage cheese
1 egg	
½ cup	parsley, chopped
¼ tsp.	salt
pepper	
nutmeg	
½ lb.	frozen phyllo dough
¾ cup	butter, melted

Force the feta cheese and the cottage cheese through a sieve with the back of a spoon. Add the parsley, salt, a few grindings of black pepper and a dash of nutmeg.

Lay a sheet of phyllo dough on the table. Brush it with butter. Put 2 tbsp. of the cheese filling on one of the short ends of the dough, covering about a third of the width of the dough, in the middle. Pick up the end that has the filling on it and roll it over twice to wrap the filling. Then fold one side over the filling and brush it with butter and then repeat the process with the other side. Now continue rolling the burag, as you would a bedroll. When it is all rolled up, brush it again with butter and place it on a baking sheet, pizza pan or baking stone. Repeat this process until all of the cheese is used up.

Bake in an oven that has been preheated to 350°. The burags should be delicately browned in about 15 minutes. Do not overcook them.

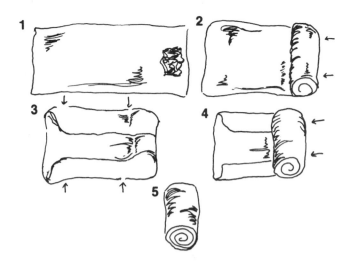

GEBACKENE KASEBROTCHEN
Germany

(Oven-Baked Sandwiches)

For six servings.

1 long loaf	French bread
¾ cup	milk
6 slices	baked ham
6 slices	Swiss, emmentaler, or gruyere cheese
2 tomatoes	dead ripe
(chopped chives)	
(chopped walnuts)	

Preheat the oven to 400°. Slice the French bread into 6 slices, 9" long and ½" thick. Dip the bread slices in milk on both sides and place them in a buttered baking pan. Put a slice of ham on each piece of bread, large enough to cover the whole slice. Cover the ham with thinly sliced tomatoes that have been drained of some of their liquid. Top with cheese.

Bake for 8 to 10 minutes, until the cheese has melted. Remove from the oven and sprinkle with either chopped chives or chopped walnuts.

OKONO MI-YAKI
Japan
(Pizza "As You Like It")

A friend of mine who has lived in Japan was told by his friends there that this is "Japanese pizza." The name of the dish gives you considerable freedom when deciding what ingredients to include. The batter is fried in vegetable oil to make individual servings like our pancakes. Some of the filling ingredients may have to be precooked. In this version, the mushrooms are partially precooked before they are placed under the batter. These "pizzas" should be accompanied by either soy sauce or a mixture of ton katsu (available in Japanese food stores) and mayonnaise. To serve four.

Batter

4 cups	shredded cabbage: oriental or American
2 cups	flour
1 cup	half and half
2 eggs	
1 carrot	grated
1 onion	grated
1 tsp.	salt

Filling

¼ lb.	fresh mushrooms, sliced
1 tomato	chopped and drained
⅛ lb.	ham, chopped
¼ cup	chopped scallion

Mix all of the batter ingredients together in a large bowl. Have the filling ingredients chopped and ready within reach while you cook. In a large frying pan, heat 2 tbsp. vegetable oil. Saute the sliced mushrooms for 4 minutes and remove them to a dish with the other filling ingredients. Put another tbsp. of oil in the pan. When the oil is hot, put 2 tsp. of the filling in a little pile in the pan. Immediately cover it with 2 tbsp. of batter. Repeat this process until you have as many little "pizzas" in the pan as it will comfortably hold. Cook for about 4 minutes per side over a medium flame. Both sides should be nicely browned when they are done. The filling will end up on top. Be sure the batter is thoroughly cooked in the middle before you remove each "pizza" from the pan. You may want to make a cut with the side of the spatula to check for doneness. Add more oil to the pan as you go along, if necessary, as you repeat the process with the remainder of the ingredients.

VATRUSHKI
Russia
(Individual Cheese Tarts)

These little tarts can be served alone or as part of a larger meal, with salads, soups, or vegetarian dishes. For sixteen 3" tartlets.

Dough

2 cups	flour
½ tsp.	baking powder
½ tsp.	salt
2 eggs	
½ cup	plain yogurt
¼ cup	butter (unsalted), softened

Sift the flour, baking powder and salt into a bowl. Add the yogurt, eggs and softened butter. With a wooden spoon, blend the ingredients together, creaming the butter into the flour with the back of the spoon. When the dough is smooth, place it in a clean bowl and refrigerate for an hour.

Filling

16 oz.	cottage cheese
1 tbsp.	plain yogurt
2 eggs	
1 tsp.	light brown sugar
½ tsp.	salt

Put the cottage cheese through a food mill or force it through a strainer with the back of a spoon. Add the yogurt, eggs, sugar, and salt. Blend the ingredients thoroughly and refrigerate for 30 minutes.

When the dough and the filling have been chilled, roll out the dough to a thickness of ⅛" on a floured board. (You will have to flour both the board and the rolling pin thoroughly because the dough tends to be sticky). Cut out 4" circles with a biscuit cutter. Roll up the edges of the circles to form a rim. Fill each of tartlets with about 2 tsp. of the cheese and egg mixture. Lift them gently onto a baking sheet with a spatula.

Glaze

1 egg

Separate the egg and beat the yolk lightly. Brush the dough with the egg yolk and bake at 400° for about 20 minutes.

GOUGERE AUX EPINARDS
France

(Spinach and Mushrooms in Cheese Pastry)

This is a pretty dish as well as a tasty one. The cheese pastry will puff up attractively and its flavor is a perfect complement to that of the vegetables. Make it in a baking dish that is 9" x 9" x 2". To serve six.

Gougere

1¼ cup	water
1 cup (8 tbsp.)	unsalted butter
½ tsp.	salt
pepper	
1¼ cup	unbleached all-purpose flour
5 eggs	
2 cups	grated Swiss cheese

Preheat the oven to 400°. Use 1 tbsp. of butter to thoroughly grease the inside of the baking dish. Put the water, butter, salt and a little pepper in a pot and bring the water to a boil. Pour in all of the flour at once and stir until the ingredients are well mixed. Put the dough in a bowl and let it cool for a few minutes, stirring all the while. Add the eggs individually, stirring each into the mixture before you add the next. Then stir in the grated Swiss cheese. When all of the ingredients are thoroughly combined, spread the mixture in the buttered baking dish. Line the bottom of the dish and the sides with the pastry. You may use your fingers or the back of a spoon to spread the mixture evenly. Bake for 20 minutes. Do not open the oven during this initial baking period.

Filling

1 lb.	fresh spinach leaves
½ lb.	fresh mushrooms
½ cup	chopped onion
4 tbsp.	unsalted butter
2 tbsp.	vegetable oil
2 tbsp.	flour
1 cup	half and half
1 large	tomato
½ lb.	Swiss cheese, sliced thin
salt and pepper	

Melt 2 tbsp. of butter and 2 tbsp. of oil in a saute pan. Saute the chopped onions over medium-high heat for 5 minutes. Wipe the mushrooms clean with a slightly damp cloth or mushroom brush and slice them thin. Add the mushrooms to the pan and saute for another 5 minutes. Season with a little salt and pepper and remove the mushrooms and onions to a bowl. Put another 2 tbsp. of butter in the pan and let it melt. Add 2 tbsp. of flour and stir with a wire whisk until the butter and flour form a smooth paste. Cook over low heat for 4 minutes, then begin to add the half and half a little at a time. Stir with the whisk constantly. When all of the half and half has been added, you will have a smooth, thick cream sauce. Put the mushrooms and onions back into the pan with the sauce.

Wash the spinach leaves thoroughly and remove the tough stems. Steam the spinach leaves for 3 minutes until they have barely wilted. Add the spinach to the creamed mushrooms. Taste for seasoning and add more salt if necessary.

Remove the gougere from the oven after it has baked for 20 minutes. You will have a puffy pastry crust. Pour the creamed spinach and mushrooms into the crust and cover with slices of tomato. Put the sliced Swiss cheese on top and bake for another 10 to 15 minutes.

CORNISH PASTIES
England

(Meat and Vegetables in Dough)

These meat-filled pastry pockets are served throughout England, and a similar dish is made in Poland and in Scandinavia. Like the calzone in Chapter IV, pasties can be made in a variety of sizes and shapes with fillings to match your taste. The recipe below is typical of what you will find in public eating houses and private homes in England. Small pasties are popular as a breakfast dish. These will be relatively large. For four pasties.

2½ cups	unbleached all-purpose flour
1 cup	lard, chilled and cut into small pieces
1 onion	diced
2 potatoes	scrubbed, dried and diced
½ cup	yellow or white turnip, diced
2 carrots	scrubbed, dried and sliced
1 lb.	lean beef, coarsely chopped
4 tbsp.	butter
cold water	
1 tsp.	salt
pepper	
1 tbsp.	vegetable oil
1 egg	

Sift the flour and salt into a bowl and cut the lard into the flour with 2 knives until the dough resembles coarse meal. Add ½ cup of cold water and work it into the dough with your fingers. If the dough does not hold together, add more water, a tablespoon at a time, until it does. Gather the dough into a ball and set it aside, covered, for an hour.

While the dough is resting, prepare the filling. Preheat the oven to 425°. Mix all of the diced vegetables, the meat and some salt and pepper in a bowl. Divide the dough into 4 equal parts. Roll each part out to a circle 9″ or so in diameter. (Use a plate or pot top placed over the dough to get the proper size. Cut around the edge with a sharp knife or pastry cutter.) Put a quarter of the filling on one side of the circle. Dot the filling with 1 tbsp. of butter, cut into pieces. Lift the other side of the dough over the filling and crimp the edges together with a fork or your fingers. Repeat this process for the other pieces of dough.

Beat together the yolk of the egg and 1 tbsp. of vegetable oil. Brush each of the pasties with this glaze. Make a few slits in the top of the dough to allow steam to escape while they are cooking.

Bake for 10 minutes at 425°; then reduce the heat to 375° and continue cooking until they are golden brown and a fork will easily pierce the vegetables inside the crust. Total cooking time is about an hour.

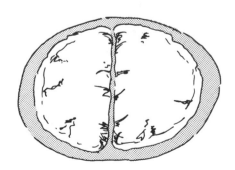

ENVUELTOS DE AGUACATE
Mexico

(Avocado Envelopes)

A quicker version of this recipe can be made as an hors d'oeuvre by piling a teaspoonful or two of guacamole onto Dorito or Tostito chips, topping them with cheese and setting them under the broiler until the cheese melts. If you make it this way, call it nachos or kamoosh, and serve it with hot pepper sauce and/or sour cream.

The guacamole can be made in advance, as much as a day ahead. If you plan to store it, put the avocado pits in the mixture and cover tightly before placing in the refrigerator. Remove the pits from the mixture only when you are ready to use it. This helps keep the guacamole from discoloring.

The recipe below can be used as a meatless entree for dinner. They are also surprisingly good reheated as leftovers. The tortilla will expand and become soft as it absorbs moisture from the sauce and filling. You may actually prefer this texture to the harder, chewier texture of the original recipe.

Guacamole filling

4	ripe avocadoes
1	lime
2	tomatoes
½ cup	chopped scallion
¼ cup	chopped parsley
¼ cup	chopped green pepper
salt	
pepper	
2 cloves	garlic

Peel and mash the avocadoes with a wooden spoon in a glass or wooden bowl. You may find it necessary to hash the avocadoes a little with 2 knives before mashing them with the spoon. Add the juice of 1 lime, the chopped scallion, parsley and green pepper. Crush the 2 cloves of garlic into the mixture with a garlic press. Remove the liquid and most of the seeds from the tomatoes and then chop up the flesh and add it to the avocado mixture. Season to taste with salt and pepper.

Tortilla wrappers and sauce

10	frozen tortillas
10 slices	monterey jack cheese
4 tbsp.	vegetable oil
3 cups	tomato sauce
1 - 2 tbsp.	chili powder
½ cup	chopped onion
¼ cup	vegetable oil

In 2 tbsp. of vegetable oil, saute the chopped onions until they are transparent. Remove from the heat, stir in the chili powder (use more or less depending on how spicy you like it) and the tomato sauce. Let the sauce simmer for 10 minutes. Meanwhile, in a small frying pan, heat the other 2 tbsp. of oil. When the oil is hot, fry the tortillas, one at a time, for about 1 minute on each side. Have the guacamole and a baking sheet or pizza pan handy as you fry the tortillas.

As each tortilla is finished, put the next one in the pan and quickly cover half of the hot tortilla with guacamole. Fold the tortilla over and place it on its side on the baking sheet. You must fill the tortillas while they are hot or they will become brittle and break when you fold them over. When all of the tortillas have been fried and filled, put a generous slice of monterey jack cheese on each. Ladle tomato sauce over the tortillas and bake at 400° for 7 to 10 minutes, until the cheese melts.

SPANAKOPITA
Greece

(Cheese and Spinach Pie with Phyllo Dough)

To make this cheese and spinach pie, you must have access to phyllo dough or strudel leaves. Theoretically, you can make these tissue-thin sheets of dough at home, but they are available in frozen form in Greek, Turkish and Armenian grocery stores and in many large supermarkets in frozen food sections with other "ethnic" foods. This recipe uses an 8" x 8" x 2" baking dish and will serve four people as a main course.

16 sheets	phyllo dough
1 lb.	fresh spinach
1 cup	chopped scallions or green onion
1 tbsp.	chopped fresh parsley
1 tbsp.	chopped fresh dill weed
6 oz.	feta cheese
2 eggs	lightly beaten
salt	
pepper	
nutmeg	
½ cup (¼ lb.)	melted butter (unsalted)
2 tbsp.	olive oil

Wash the spinach thoroughly, and dry. Remove the tough stems and chop. Saute the chopped scallion in olive oil for 4 minutes, then add the chopped spinach. Cover and cook over medium-low heat for 5 minutes. Meanwhile, mash the feta cheese in a bowl and stir in the lightly beaten eggs, ¾ tsp. salt, a few grindings of pepper and a dash of ground nutmeg. Blend the cheese, eggs, and spices thoroughly. Remove the cover from the spinach and add the chopped dill and the chopped parsley. Cook uncovered for 2 or 3 more minutes. There should be no liquid left in the pan at this point. Drain the greens, if necessary. Place them in a large bowl and spread the mixture along the sides of the bowl so it will cool rapidly. Place the bowl in the refrigerator while you begin to assemble the dough in the baking pan. The greens should be somewhat cooled before you add the cheese and egg mixture.

Brush the baking pan with some of the melted butter. Then place a sheet of phyllo in the pan. Fit the dough to the contours of the pan and then brush it with butter. Repeat this process until you have 8 sheets of dough in the baking pan. Add the cheese mixture to the spinach and combine thoroughly. Spread this mixture on top of the dough. Be sure you make an even layer that reaches into each corner of the baking pan. Cover the spinach and cheese with a layer of phyllo and brush it with butter. Repeat until you have used another 8 sheets of dough. Trim the excess dough with kitchen scissors.

Place the spanakopita in a 325° oven for about 50 minutes. The crust should be delicately browned. Let the pie cool for a few minutes after you remove it from the oven before cutting. Cut into squares to serve.

PIEROGI
Poland

(Stuffed Breads)

Pierogi can be stuffed with vegetables, meat, or cheese. They can be steamed, fried, or baked. The recipes below were chosen because they use ingredients that are similar to those used in pizzas; that is, cheese and mushrooms. For about two dozen.

Dough and glaze

1 recipe	brioche pizza dough (p. 23)
1 egg	
1 tbsp.	vegetable oil

Cheese filling

8 oz.	cottage cheese
4 oz.	cream cheese
¼ cup	sour cream
1 egg	
1 tsp.	light brown sugar
1 tsp.	salt
nutmeg	
2 tbsp.	chopped chives

Force the cottage cheese through a sieve with the back of a spoon into a bowl. Blend in the cream cheese, sour cream, sugar, a dash of nutmeg and 2 tbsp. chopped chives. Fill the pierogi according to the instructions below.

Mushroom filling

1 lb.	fresh mushrooms
1 cup	chopped onion
2 tbsp.	butter
1 tbsp.	vegetable oil
2 eggs	hard boiled and chopped
¼ cup	sour cream
½ cup	bread crumbs
1 tsp.	salt
pepper	

Heat the butter and oil together and saute the chopped onion for 5 minutes over medium-high heat. Wipe the mushrooms clean with a damp cloth or mushroom brush and chop them. Add to the onions and saute for 5 minutes more. Remove from the heat, stir in the sour cream, chopped hard boiled eggs, bread crumbs and seasonings. Fill the pierogi according to the instructions below.

Assembling the pierogi. After the dough has risen for 2 hours (see recipe), roll it out to a thickness of about ⅛". Cut the dough into 4" rounds and place 2 to 3 tbsp. of the filling somewhat off center on the dough. Lift the dough over the filling and seal the edges by pinching them together with your fingers. Place the pierogi on a buttered (or oiled) baking sheet or pizza pan and cover with a towel. Allow them to rise for 20 minutes. Preheat the oven to 400°. Mix the egg with 1 tbsp. of vegetable oil and brush the pierogi with it as a glaze. Bake for 15 to 20 minutes, until the pierogi are golden brown.

QUICHE
France

(Cheese and Vegetable Pie)

Like pizza itself, quiche can be made to suit your own taste. You can make it with ham, crumbled bits of bacon, mushrooms, spinach, olives, seafood--anything that goes well with cheese. I have selected this recipe because it uses the same combination of ingredients (cheese, onions and tomatoes) as classic pizza. You can make quiche in a quiche pan or in a regular pie pan. This recipe is for a 9" pie pan. It is so good, you should probably make two at a time. If there is any left over, you can eat it cold for breakfast, lunch or snacks.

Pate brisee (pie crust pastry)

1 cup	flour
¼ tsp.	salt
⅓ cup	cold butter, unsalted
⅓ cup	ice water

Sift the flour and salt into a bowl. Cut the cold butter into small pieces and drop them into the flour. With 2 sharp knives cut the butter into the flour until the mixture has the appearance of coarse meal. Add the ice water and stir the ingredients with a fork. When the mixture can be gathered into a ball, stop adding water. Wrap the ball of dough in waxed paper and keep it in the refrigerator for 2 hours.

After the dough has chilled, roll it out on a lightly floured board until it is slightly larger than your pie pan or quiche pan. Roll the dough up on the rolling pin and unroll it carefully onto the pan. Gently ease the dough against the sides of the pan by lifting the excess that hangs over the sides and pressing the slack against the pan. This dough is not elastic like bread dough; don't try to stretch it. When the dough has been fitted to the pan, cut off the overhanging part with a very sharp knife. The crust will shrink a little, so don't cut the pastry too close to the edge of the pan.

Preheat the oven to 450°. Place a piece of aluminum foil over the pastry and cover the bottom with raw rice or beans to hold the crust down while it bakes. Bake for 8 to 10 minutes and then remove the rice or beans and aluminum foil. Continue baking for another 4 minutes. Remove the pie shell and let it cool somewhat before adding the filling.

Cheese, onion and tomato filling

1 cup	chopped onion
1½ tbsp.	butter
2 cups	grated Swiss cheese
½ cup	freshly grated parmesan cheese
1½ tsp.	flour
1 cup	half and half
2 eggs	
nutmeg	
salt	
pepper	
1 large or 2 small	fresh, ripe tomatoes

Saute the chopped onion in the butter for 6 minutes until it is clear but not browned. Add a little salt and pepper to the onions. Combine the grated cheeses and the flour thoroughly. Beat the eggs lightly in a bowl and add the half and half, a little salt and a pinch of nutmeg. Beat the custard ingredients together. When the pie shell has cooled slightly, turn the oven down to 400° and spread the sauted onions on the bottom of the crust. Cover the onions with the cheese mixture and pour the custard on top. Slice the tomatoes and place them on top of the quiche. Sprinkle a little more salt on the top and a few grindings of pepper.

Bake at 400° for 15 minutes and then reduce the heat to 325° and bake for an additional 30 minutes. The top of the quiche should be delicately browned. You may test for doneness by inserting a knife into the middle of the quiche. If the knife comes up clean, your quiche is ready to eat.

FELAFEL
Israel

(Pita Bread Stuffed with Spiced Chickpea Balls)

Felafel may be served by itself as an appetizer or for lunch, but it is best known as a filling for pita bread. Chopped tomato should be used in the sandwich with the felafel. Serve hot from the pan or save in the refrigerator for cold pita sandwiches. To fill eight pita breads.

1 recipe	pita bread (p. 24)
2 ripe tomatoes	chopped
2 cans	garbanzo beans or
(15 oz. each)	chick peas
3 tbsp.	lemon juice
½ cup	cracked wheat
2 cloves	garlic
1 slice	bread
1½ tsp.	cumin
1½ tsp.	coriander
pepper	
2 tsp.	salt
⅓ cup	chopped fresh parsley
½ cup	cooking oil

Soak the cracked wheat in water for 20 minutes, then drain and dry thoroughly. While the wheat is soaking, rinse the beans well and grind them either in a large mortar and pestle or in a food mill, electric grinder or blender. If you use a hand food mill, put the beans through twice. Soak the bread slice in water for a few minutes and then squeeze out as much of the water as possible. Add the spices and parsley to the bean paste and crush the garlic into the mixture with a garlic press. Work the seasonings thoroughly into the ground beans. Add the drained wheat and bread. Mix these ingredients thoroughly.

Shape the mixture into small balls, about ¾" in diameter and set aside on a platter uncovered for about 1½ hours. They should lose some of their moisture during this time which will help them fry properly.

When the felafel balls have dried, heat the oil in a large frying pan until it is very hot, but not smoking. Cook the balls in the oil a few at a time, turning them carefully so they will stay whole while browning on all sides. Transfer the browned felafel balls to a warm platter until all of them have been cooked.

Open the pita breads and stuff them with the felafel balls and add chopped fresh tomatoes.

HAE KUNG
Thailand

(Little Shrimp Pies)

You can make 16 half-moon pies or eight full-moon pies with this recipe. If you make the whole circles, the cooking time should be slightly longer because you will have more stuffing inside, and you will want to be sure that the shrimp gets cooked thoroughly.

Dough

3 oz.	cream cheese
¼ lb.	unsalted butter, softened
1 cup	flour

Cut the cream cheese into the flour and add the softened butter. Continue to cut the ingredients together with 2 knives until it has the appearance of coarse cornmeal. Gather the pastry into a loose ball. If the pastry is too dry to stay in a ball, add water, a teaspoon at a time. When the dough forms a cohesive ball, wrap it in waxed paper and chill for an hour.

Filling

¼ lb.	green (uncooked) shrimp
1 clove	garlic
1 tbsp.	flour
2 tbsp.	scallions, chopped
2 tbsp.	melted butter
1 egg	
½ tsp.	salt
pepper	

Peel, devein, and chop the raw shrimp. Combine it in a bowl with 1 clove of crushed garlic, the scallions, flour, egg, salt and pepper.

Assembling the Hae Kung. Roll out the dough (you will probably have to do it in several batches) to a thickness of ⅛". Cut into 3" rounds with a biscuit cutter. To make half-moon pies, put as much filling as you can on half of the dough and lift the other side over the filling to make a fat little stuffed pocket. Pinch the edges of the dough together to seal in the stuffing. If the stuffing won't stay inside, you have used too much.

To make circular pies, place the filling over a whole circle, leaving only a little edge, and place a second circle of pastry on top. Seal the edges with your fingers or a fork.

Bake the pies at 350°. The half moons take 20 minutes, the full moons take 25 to 30 minutes.

GIBANICA
Serbia
(Soft Cheese Pie)

If you only like the flavor of the soft inside of brie or camembert cheese, cut the rind away carefully and exclude it from this dish. Like many cheese and pastry dishes, this is delicious as a cold left-over as well as hot from the oven. For six to eight servings.

12 sheets	phyllo dough
½ cup (¼ lb.)	melted butter (unsalted)
½ lb.	ripe brie or camembert cheese
½ lb.	cream cheese
5 eggs	
2 cups	half and half
salt	
cream of tartar	

Brush a baking dish with melted butter. Soften the cream cheese and then blend it into the brie or camembert. Separate the eggs and blend the yolks into the cheeses. Beat the whites until they are foamy. Add a pinch of salt and a pinch of cream of tartar. Continue beating until stiff peaks form. Fold the beaten egg whites into the cheese mixture, then add the half and half with ½ to 1 tsp. of salt.

Dip a sheet of phyllo into the mixture and lay it in the baking pan. Repeat this process until you have 6 sheets piled on top of each other. Then pour the rest of the cheese mixture into the baking dish. Cover with a sheet of phyllo, and brush it with butter. Repeat this process for the remaining sheets of phyllo, brushing each with butter. Pierce the dough with a sharp knife in 2 or 3 places. Trim the edges and bake at 400° for 35 to 40 minutes. The crust should be lightly browned. Do not overcook.

MANTARH BOREK
Turkey
(Cheese and Mushrooms Baked in Dough)

For six servings.

12 sheets	phyllo dough
¾ cup (1½ sticks)	butter
1 tbsp.	vegetable oil
1 onion	finely chopped
1 lb.	fresh mushrooms
1 tbsp.	chopped fresh dill
2 tbsp.	flour
½ cup	half and half
½ cup	milk
¼ cup	grated kasari or cheddar cheese
salt	
pepper	

Melt 2 tbsp. of butter in a saucepan and slowly add the flour, stirring constantly with a wire whisk. When a smooth paste forms, cook over low heat for 5 minutes, stirring constantly. Add the half and half a little at a time, still stirring. Then add the milk. The sauce will thicken as it warms. Add the grated cheese and salt and pepper to taste. The cheese will melt into the sauce. Set this aside.

Melt 2 tbsp. of butter and 1 tbsp. of vegetable oil in a saute pan. Add the chopped onions and cook over moderate heat for about 5 minutes. Wipe the mushrooms clean with a damp cloth and slice. Cook them over medium-high heat for 5 minutes. Add the mushrooms and onions to the cheese sauce. Divide the filling into 6 portions.

Assembling the borek. First place a sheet of phyllo dough on the table. Brush it with melted butter. Put a second sheet of dough over the first and brush it with butter. Put a portion of the filling in the middle of the dough. Fold one side of the dough over the filling and brush it with butter. Take the opposite side and fold it over the filling; brush with butter. Repeat for the third and fourth sides until you have a square package of filled, buttered dough. Place the package on a buttered baking sheet, pizza pan or baking tile and repeat the process until you have used the 12 sheets of phyllo and all of the filling. Spread the remaining butter on top of the borek.

Bake at 350° for 25 to 30 minutes. The borek should be a light golden brown. The texture will suffer if overcooked.

KHACHAPURI
Russia
(Cheese-filled bread)

For four breads.

1 cup	unbleached all-purpose flour
½ cup	warm (not hot) milk
1 pkg.	yeast
2 tsp.	light brown sugar
1 tsp.	salt
7 tbsp.	soft butter
1 lb.	munster or other mild-flavored cheese, grated
2 eggs	

Dissolve the sugar and yeast in the warm milk and let it stand for 5 minutes in a warm place. Be sure the milk is not too hot, or the yeast will not become active. Sift the flour and salt into a bowl and add 4 tbsp. butter and the yeast mixture. Mix the ingredients together thoroughly and then knead them on a floured board for 8 to 10 minutes until the dough is smooth and stretchy. Place the dough in a clean bowl and brush the top with ½ tbsp. melted butter. Cover the bowl with a towel and place it in a warm, draft-free place for 1 hour. Punch down the dough and let it rise for another 45 minutes.

While the dough is rising, prepare the filling. Combine the grated cheese, 2 tbsp. of soft butter and 1 egg in a bowl. Beat them together until the mixture is well blended.

When the dough has risen for the second time, divide it into 4 equal parts and roll each out to a thickness of about ⅛". Place a quarter of the cheese mixture in the center of each piece of dough. Gather the edges of the dough to the center and pinch together to seal in the cheese. Let the filled breads rise for 15 more minutes on a buttered baking sheet.

Preheat the oven to 375°. Separate an egg and beat the yolk with the remaining soft butter. Brush the breads with this glaze just before baking. Bake for 25 to 30 minutes until golden brown.

PISSALADIERE
France
(Provincial Onion Pizza)

A direct descendent of the original Roman pizza, this French provincial dish can be made with or without tomatoes. Because it is a true cousin of the popular Neopolitan and American pizza, the name "pissaladiere" is giving way to the name "pizza provencale." For one 14" pizza.

½ recipe	basic pizza dough (p. 14)
½ cup	olive oil
2 large	bermuda onions
2 cloves	garlic
(2 tomatoes)	
12 fillets	flat anchovy
⅔ cup	stoned black olives
salt	
pepper	

Slice the bermuda onions and cook them in a large frying pan in 1/3 cup of oil until they are transparent. Do not let them brown. Crush the garlic into the onions and cook for another 5 minutes over a medium-low heat. If you want to add tomatoes, chop them coarsely and drain out most of the juice. Add the tomatoes to the onions and cook for an additional 2 or 3 minutes. Stir in salt and pepper to taste, but bear in mind that you will be covering the mixture with anchovies which will add considerable saltiness to the finished dish.

When the dough has risen for 1½ hours, roll it out and slip it onto a pizza pan, baking sheet or pizza stone which has been sprinkled with cornmeal. Roll up the edge of the dough to form a rim. Brush the dough with the remaining olive oil and spread the onion mixture over it. Drain the anchovies thoroughly of oil and place them in a criss-cross pattern over the onions. Slice the olives and put the slices in the grid that is formed by the anchovies. Cover the pissaladiere with a clean cloth and let it rise for 15 to 20 minutes. While it is rising, preheat the oven to 400°. Bake for 25 to 30 minutes, keeping an eye on the crust after 20 minutes to be sure it doesn't get overdone.

PYRISZHKY
Russia
(Mushroom-Stuffed Breads)

These little breads are very much like stuffed pizza pockets or calzone. The filling for pyriszhky, however, is fairly bland. You will enjoy them as an accompaniment to hot, strongly flavored soup or salads made with sharp-tasting vegetables or greens, such as radishes or watercress. They may be served as a lunch, brunch, or first course with sour cream or wedges of cheese. For 16 pyriszhky.

½ recipe	basic pizza dough (p. 14)
4 tbsp.	sweet butter
1 lb.	fresh mushrooms
¾ cup	chopped scallions or green onions
¾ - 1 tsp.	salt
black pepper	
½ cup	cooked brown rice
2 eggs	hard boiled and chopped
3 tbsp.	chopped fresh parsley
1 egg yolk	
4 tbsp.	vegetable oil

While the dough is rising, prepare the filling. Melt the butter and 2 tbsp. of vegetable oil in a saute pan. When the oil is hot, add the chopped scallions and mushrooms. Cook over a medium heat for 5 minutes. Add the salt and pepper and then transfer to a bowl. Add the cooked rice and the chopped hard boiled eggs and allow the ingredients to cool slightly. Then add the chopped parsley.

When the dough has risen for 1½ hours, preheat the oven to 350°. Divide the dough into 16 pieces. Roll out each piece to make a circle 5" in diameter. Divide the filling into 16 equal parts and place each portion on one side of a piece of dough. Fold the opposite side of the dough over the filling, and pinch the edges together with a fork. Repeat the process until you have 16 stuffed semi-circles. Place the pyriszhky on a baking sheet.

Mix the egg yolk with the 2 remaining tbsp. of vegetable oil. With a pastry brush, paint the glaze on each of the breads. Bake at 350° for 20 to 25 minutes, until they are golden brown.

VI

MUD PIES

Recipes For Kids

This chapter features recipes that kids can make. They range from 15 minute quickies to projects that take several hours from beginning to end. Children should learn to read a recipe thoroughly and consider the time factor involved before they begin to cook. Grown-ups can make these recipes also, either for their children or for themselves.

A number of the recipes in this chapter can be used to turn a child's birthday party into a real event. Put the dough and ingredients out on the table and let the children roll out the dough and create their own pizzas. This can be a little messy, perhaps, but it's a really delightful way for children to begin their cooking careers.

Ask any child what his or her favorite foods are and undoubtedly, pizza will be at the top of the list. By now, you have seen that pizza is a dish of tremendous range and versatility, truly deserving of the gourmet's "cordon bleu." However, there is still much to be said for the joys of good old kids' pizza.

PITA PIZZA

You can make pizza with pita bread either by splitting it in half like an English muffin or by stuffing the pizza ingredients inside the pocket.

You can buy pita bread frozen in the store, but it is more fun to make your own. Heat from the oven makes the pita puff up and form the pocket, so be sure you have the oven well preheated before you bake the dough.

Read the recipe carefully before you start to work. Pita has to rise several different times before you can put it in the oven. Figure out how much time to allow from beginning to end. The recipe for pita is on page 24. That recipe makes eight pita breads. This recipe uses four.

4 loaves	pita bread, commercial or homemade
1 cup	pizza sauce
½ lb.	mozzarella cheese, sliced or grated
½ cup	grated parmesan cheese
2 tsp.	dried oregano
1 tsp.	garlic salt
2 tbsp.	olive oil

Heat the oven to 400°. Slice the pitas in half as you would a roll or an English muffin, and place them on a baking sheet with the inside facing up. Brush a little olive oil on each and place in the oven for 2 minutes. Remove the baking sheet and spoon 1 tbsp. of sauce over each pita. Distribute the mozzarella cheese and grated parmesan over each. Sprinkle with garlic salt and dried oregano. Dribble the remaining olive oil over the top. Return them to the oven and bake for 8 minutes more, until the cheese has thoroughly melted.

MINIATURE DEEP-DISH PIZZA

Save up the tins from frozen pot pies, and you can make little deep-dish pizzas in them, either single crust or double crust. The recipe below will make eight double crust miniature pizzas. If you want single crust pizzas, just make half of the recipe.

Equipment you will need
sifter
measuring cup and spoons
large bowl
kneading board
clean dish towel
rolling pin
8 tins from frozen pot pies
pastry brush or paper towels
kitchen scissors

Ingredients

4½ cups	unbleached all-purpose flour
1 tsp.	salt
2 pkg.	dry yeast
1½ cups	warm water
2 tsp.	sugar
4 tbsp. (¼ cup)	vegetable oil
1 cup	pizza sauce
½ lb.	mozzarella cheese, grated or sliced
½ cup	grated parmesan cheese
1 tsp.	dried oregano
1 tsp.	garlic salt
(green pepper)	
(sliced onion)	
(pepperoni)	
(mushrooms)	
(olives)	

First make the dough. Measure ½ cup of warm water in a measuring cup. Be sure that the water is just warm. If the water is hot, it will kill the yeast and the dough won't rise. Put 2 tsp. of sugar and the dry yeast in the warm water and stir until it is dissolved. Let the yeast mixture rest for at least 5 minutes. You will begin to see the yeast becoming active when the mixture gets foamy.

Meanwhile, sift 4 cups of flour in a large bowl with 1 tsp. of salt. Make a hole in the middle of the flour and put in 3 tbsp. of vegetable oil and 1 cup of water. When the yeast mixture is ready, add it to the flour. Mix all of the ingredients together with a large spoon or with your hands. If the dough sticks to your hands, a little flour will help get it off.

Put some flour on the kneading board and put the dough out onto it. Knead the dough for 5 minutes. There is a picture of how to knead dough on page 14. You have to push the dough with your hands and fold it back onto itself until it is well mixed. When you are finished kneading, the dough should be stretchy and smooth. If the dough is too sticky, you can add a little flour.

Wash out the mixing bowl and brush it with vegetable oil. Put the ball of kneaded dough into the bowl and cover it with a clean dish towel.

Place the bowl in a warm, draft-free place for 1½ hours to rise.

While the dough is rising, you can get everything else ready. Make your own sauce if you want to (see recipe p. 27), or use a commercially prepared sauce. Slice up the ingredients that you are going to use to fill your pizza. Grate or slice the mozzarella cheese. Have everything prepared by the time the dough is ready to be rolled out.

Assembling the pizzas. After the dough has risen for 1½ hours, preheat the oven to 400°. Take a small piece of dough and put it on the floured board. Put flour on your rolling pin and roll the dough out until it is large enough to fill the baking tin. The dough should hang over the edge of the tin a little. Trim the dough with kitchen scissors if it hangs over too much. If you are making single crust pizzas, put 1 tbsp. of pizza sauce on the dough, add your favorite filling ingredients and cover with grated or sliced mozzarella cheese. Sprinkle with dried oregano, a little garlic salt, and some parmesan cheese. Bake for 20 minutes.

If you are making double crust pizzas, first follow the directions above. When your pizza is assembled, roll out another piece of dough and place it over the baking tin. Pinch the 2 pieces of dough together and trim the excess with kitchen scissors. Bake for 20 minutes.

VALENTINE'S DAY PIZZA

You can make this big red heart for Valentine's Day. It is a beautiful pizza and sure to let your loved one know how much you care. Once you have made this pizza, you will probably think of other shapes you would like to make. There is really no reason why pizzas have to be round or rectangular. You could make a green clover-leaf shaped pizza for St. Patrick's Day using the spinach dough on page 20. Try forming your initials in pizza dough. Instead of a gingerbread man you can make a "pizza person," and so on.

Equipment you will need
  measuring cup and spoons
  large bowl
  kneading board
  clean dish towel
  rolling pin
  pizza pan or baking sheet
  knife or pizza wheel
  pastry brush or paper towels

Ingredients
2½ cups	unbleached all-purpose flour
½ tsp.	salt
1 pkg.	dry yeast
¼ cup	warm water
1 tsp.	sugar
2½ tsp.	vegetable oil
2 cups (16 oz.)	pizza sauce
1½ cups	grated mozzarella cheese
¼ cup	grated parmesan cheese
2 slices	salami

Remember, you have to allow 1½ hours for the dough to rise. You cannot use a commercially prepared dough for this special pizza.

First make the dough. Measure ¼ cup of warm water in a measuring cup. Be sure that the water is just warm; hot water will kill the yeast and the dough won't rise. Put a tsp. of sugar and the dry yeast in the water and stir until they are dissolved. Let the yeast mixture rest undisturbed for at least 5 minutes. You will begin to see evidence of the yeast becoming active as the mixture gets foamy.

Meanwhile, sift 2 cups of flour into a large bowl with ½ tsp. of salt. Make a hole in the middle of the flour and put in 4 tsp. of vegetable oil and 1 cup of the pizza sauce. When the yeast mixture is ready add it to the flour, too. Mix all the ingredients together with a large spoon or with your hands. If the dough sticks to your hands, a little flour will help get it off.

Put some flour on your kneading board and put the dough out onto it. Knead the dough for about 8 minutes. There is a picture of how to knead dough on page 14. You have to push the dough with your hands and fold it back onto itself until it is well mixed. When you are finished kneading, the dough should be stretchy and smooth. If the dough is too sticky while you are kneading it, add just a little bit of flour. If it is too stiff, add just a little bit of water.

Wash the bowl and rub a small amount of vegetable oil in it. Place the ball of kneaded dough into the bowl and cover with a clean dish towel. Put the bowl in a warm, draft-free place for 1½ hours. When the time is up, you can assemble your pizza.

While the dough is rising, you can get the other ingredients ready. This shouldn't take very long. Grate the mozzarella cheese and the parmesan cheese and set them aside in a bowl. Slice the pieces of salami so that one piece looks like the back end of an arrow and the other piece looks like the front end of an arrow. Wrap them up and save for later.

Assembling the pizza. When the dough has risen for 1½ hours, put flour on the board and on your rolling pin. Put the dough on the board and roll it out into a large circle that is the same size as your pizza pan. Now take a pizza wheel or sharp knife and cut out a heart shape in the dough. Make it as big as you can. If you have trouble doing this free-hand, you can cut out a paper heart and lay it over the dough as a pattern. If your first attempt fails, you can always gather up the dough into a ball again and reroll it.

Now you have to make the rim. Take the scraps of dough that you have cut away and cut them into wide strips. Roll the strips in your hands to make long "snakes." Dip your finger in a bowl of water and paint the water around the edge of the pizza. Now fit the dough "snakes" all around the edge, pinching the rim and the heart together. You will see that the water acts like glue and the rim attaches on very easily in this way. After the heart-shaped dough is all ready, cover it with the towel and let it rise for 15 minutes.

Preheat the oven to 400°. Brush the dough with 1 tbsp. of vegetable oil. Spread 1 cup of pizza sauce over the dough and cover with the grated cheeses. Put your salami arrow on the pizza with the front end separated from the back end. Bake for 20 minutes and amaze your valentine!

PIZZA DOGS

Sloppy--but worth it. To make 12.

12	hot dogs
12	hot dog buns
12 slices	mozzarella cheese
1 can (8 oz.)	pizza sauce
1 tbsp.	dried oregano

Boil the hot dogs for 10 minutes and drain off the water. Let them cool for a few minutes before you try to handle them.

Heat the oven to 400°. (If you are only making a few pizza dogs, you can make them in a toaster oven.) Open the hot dog buns and arrange them on a baking sheet with the inside part facing up. Put a large slice of mozzarella cheese on each bun. Put the boiled hot dogs on another baking sheet. Make a slit in each one the long way, but don't cut it all the way through. Spoon about 1½ tsp. of pizza sauce into each of the hot dogs.

Put the hot dogs and the buns in the oven and cook for about 8 minutes. The cheese should be melted when you take them out of the oven. Put the hot dogs on the buns and sprinkle each with a little dried oregano.

PIZZA A LA HOT DOG

Read the whole recipe before you begin to work. The pizza dough takes 90 minutes to rise, so be sure you leave yourself enough time. You should probably allow two and a half hours from start to finish. For two 12" pizzas.

Equipment you will need
measuring cup and spoons
sifter
rolling pin
2 pizza pans or baking sheets
large bowl
clean dish towel
kneading board
sharp knife or pizza

Ingredients

4½ cups	unbleached all-purpose white flour
1 tsp.	salt
¼ cup (4 tbsp.)	vegetable oil
2 pkgs.	dry yeast
1½ cups	warm water
2 tsp.	sugar
2 cups	pizza sauce, canned or homemade (see p. 27)
1 lb.	mozzarella cheese, thinly sliced or grated
1 cup	grated parmesan or romano cheese
6 hot dogs	sliced into circles
2 tbsp.	vegetable oil

First make the dough. Measure ½ cup of warm water in a measuring cup. Don't use hot water or you will kill the yeast and the dough won't rise. If the water feels a little warmer than the air, it is probably just right. Put the 2 tsp. of sugar and the dry yeast in the warm water and stir until they dissolve. Let the yeast mixture sit undisturbed for at least 5 minutes so the yeast can become active. You will begin to see evidence of this activity when the yeast gets foamy.

Meanwhile, measure 4 cups of flour and sift them into a large bowl with 1 tsp. of salt. Make a hole in the middle of the flour and put 3 tbsp. of vegetable oil in the hole. Now put 1 cup of warm water in the hole. Add the yeast when it is ready. Mix all of the ingredients together with a spoon or your hands. If the dough sticks to your hands too much, a little flour will help get it off. When the ingredients are all mixed together and the dough can be gathered into a ball, spread ½ cup of flour on the kneading board. Put the dough on the floured board and knead it for 5 minutes. There is a picture of how to knead dough on page 14. You have to push the dough with your hands and fold it back onto itself. Knead the dough until it is stretchy and smooth.

When the dough is kneaded, you will be able to gather it up into a nice, neat ball. Brush some of the remaining oil in a large, clean bowl and place the ball of dough in it. Brush the rest of the oil onto the top of the dough ball. Cover the bowl with a clean dish towel and place it in a warm, draft-free place for 1½ hours. When the time is up, you can make your pizzas.

While you are waiting for the dough to rise you can get the other ingredients ready. You have time to make your own tomato sauce if you want to. If you are using commercially prepared sauce, you have nothing to do but cut up the ingredients that will go on top of your pizza. Cut up the cheese and the hot dogs. You can, of course, add anything else that you like on pizza, such as green peppers, olives, onions, or mushrooms. Have everything ready to go when the time comes to roll out the dough.

Assembling the pizza. When the dough has risen for 1½ hours, preheat the oven to 450°. Divide the dough into 2 equal parts and shape each part into a ball. Put flour on the board and on your rolling pin. Put 1 ball of dough on the board and flatten it with your hand. Then roll the dough into a big circle. Roll from the center of the dough out to the edge. Rotate the dough frequently to keep the circle as nearly round as possible.

When the circle is a little bigger than your pizza pan, slip the dough onto the pan. Then roll up the edge of the dough to form a rim. Roll out the second ball of dough in the same way.

Brush each of the pizzas with a tbsp. of vegetable oil. Spread 1 cup of pizza sauce on each. Dot the pizzas with the sliced hot dogs (and any other toppings you have decided on), and spread the mozzarella and parmesan cheeses over the top. Bake for 20 minutes. When they are done, the pizza crusts should be golden brown.

WHATSA MATZAH PIZZA?

A matzah pizza is a pizza that you can eat during Passover or any other time you want a quick pizza snack. For two people.

2 matzahs	
8 tsp.	pizza sauce
8 slices	mozzarella or American cheese

oregano
garlic powder

Optional, your choice of:

chopped pepper
chopped onion
bologna or salami
sliced hot dog

Break the matzahs into 4 pieces. Put them on a baking sheet so you don't get crumbs all over the oven. If you use a toaster oven, put them on a sheet of aluminum foil.

Spread 1 tsp. of pizza sauce on each piece of matzah. Add whatever else you want from the optional ingredients, and then cover with a piece of cheese. Sprinkle some dried oregano and a tiny bit of garlic powder on top.

Heat the oven to 450°. Cook the matzah pizzas for about 6 minutes, until the cheese melts.

STRAWBERRY SHORTCAKE PIZZA

This is a beautiful dessert that is a special treat for a pizza-lover. It will look like a pizza, but taste like strawberry shortcake. Allow enough time for the crust to cool completely before you put the whipped cream on it. If there is room in your refrigerator, the crust will cool in there quite quickly. For one 12" pizza.

Equipment you will need
large strainer
3 bowls
measuring cups and spoons
sifter
kneading board
pizza pan
pie place, pot top, or oven proof plate
pot holder
electric beater or hand beater
pizza wheel or sharp knife

Ingredients

2 cups	unbleached all-purpose flour
8 oz. (1 container)	plain yogurt
1 tbsp.	baking powder
1 egg	
4 tbsp.	vegetable oil
½ tsp.	salt
20 oz.	frozen strawberries or fresh ones, if possible
2 cups	whipping cream
4 tbsp.	confectioner's sugar
1 tsp.	vanilla

If you are using frozen strawberries, defrost them in a strainer over a bowl. The juice should be drained from the strawberries and reserved. If you are lucky enough to have fresh strawberries, wash some to use whole, and mash others up with some brown sugar in a bowl to serve separately as a sauce.

The crust. Preheat the oven to 450°. Sift the flour into a large bowl, add the yogurt, baking powder, egg and vegetable oil. Mix the ingredients together and turn them out onto a well-floured board. Knead the dough for 2 or 3 minutes, adding more flour if necessary. There is a picture of how to knead dough on page 14. When you are finished kneading, the dough should be elastic and smooth. Then put flour on a rolling pin and roll the dough out until it is larger than your pizza pan. Dust the pan with flour and slip the dough onto it. Roll up the edges of the dough to make a rim. Place an oven-proof object on the dough to keep it from bubbling up while it is cooking. You may use a pie plate, a pot top, or an oven-proof plate. Place the crust in the preheated oven and bake for 15 minutes. Remove the cooked crust and take the weight off of it. Remember, the weight will be hot, so use a pot holder. Allow the crust to cool thoroughly.

The whipped cream. Whip the heavy cream until the beaters begin to leave patterns in it. Then add the confectioner's sugar and the vanilla and continue whipping. The cream is finished when it doesn't drip off the beaters when you lift them. If you are whipping the cream with a hand beater, don't be surprised if it takes a long time and a lot of energy. It helps if the bowl and the beaters are chilled before you begin.

Assembling the pizza. When the crust is cooled, the cream whipped, and the strawberries defrosted and drained, you are ready to assemble your pizza.

Spread the crust with the whipped cream using a knife or a rubber spatula. Place the whole strawberries all over the whipped cream. If you are not going to serve it right away, be sure to cover the pizza and place it immediately in the refrigerator.

To serve the pizza, cut it with a pizza wheel and then spoon some of the extra strawberry juice that you have reserved over each individual piece.

PIZZA CASSEROLE

This is a good dish for dinner that the whole family will enjoy. To serve six as a main course.

1 lb.	ground hamburger meat
2 cups (16 oz.)	pizza sauce, homemade or canned
½ box (4 oz.)	macaroni shells
½ cup	half and half
8 oz.	mozzarella cheese
2 oz.	grated parmesan cheese
2 tsp.	dried oregano
1 tsp.	garlic salt
½ tsp.	butter

In a large saucepan, bring 2 quarts of water and 1 tsp. of salt to a boil. When the water boils, put half of an 8 oz. box of macaroni shells into the water. Reduce the heat so the water stays at a steady boil for 12 minutes. Stir the shells from time to time. Meanwhile, prepare the meat and sauce.

In a large frying pan, brown the hamburger meat over a medium flame. Chop the meat up with a spoon as it browns. When the meat is cooked, drain off most of the fat that has come out and throw it away. Stir the pizza sauce into the meat and add the garlic salt and oregano. Set aside.

When the shells have boiled for 12 minutes, drain them in a colander. Put the drained shells in a bowl and stir the half and half into them. Slice the mozzarella cheese into thin slices. Preheat the oven to 350°. Lightly butter the bottom and sides of a 2 quart casserole. Pour half of the meat sauce into the bottom of it. Spread half of the cooked macaroni shells on top of the sauce and then distribute half of the slices of mozzarella cheese over the shells. Repeat the process making a second layer.

Bake the casserole covered (if your casserole doesn't have a cover, use a sheet of aluminum foil) for 20 minutes. Then uncover, sprinkle the grated parmesan cheese on top and continue cooking for another 5 to 10 minutes.

When you serve the pizza casserole, try to spoon it out in such a way that the layers stay together. But if it all mixes up, don't worry because it will taste just as good.

PIZZA BURGERS

Here are the world's two best foods rolled into one. You don't have to decide whether you want a hamburger or a pizza--make a pizza burger! To make eight burgers.

2 lbs.	ground round or chuck
1 can (8 oz.)	pizza sauce
8 slices	mozzarella cheese
1 tsp.	garlic salt
2 tsp.	dried oregano
½ cup	grated parmesan cheese
8 large	hamburger buns

Heat the oven to 400°. Divide the meat into 8 equal portions and shape them into hamburgers. Pinch up some of the meat from the top edge of the hamburgers to form a rim. The rim holds in the sauce and the cheese, just like the crust on a pizza. Put the hamburgers on a baking sheet.

Spoon a tbsp. of sauce onto the top of the meat. Sprinkle a little of the garlic salt and a little of the oregano on each. Put the burgers in the oven and cook for 7 minutes. After they are partially cooked, open the oven, and slide the rack out carefully. Place a slice of mozzarella cheese on top of each burger. Return them to the oven and continue cooking for another 7 minutes.

When the pizza burgers are done and have been removed from the oven, sprinkle the tops with a little grated parmesan cheese. Put them on the buns and eat.

PIZZA BAGELS

You can make these treats with English muffins as well as with bagels; the recipe is the same. Be sure you let them cool off a little before you sink your teeth into them. The sauce gets very hot. For 10 pizza bagels.

5 bagels	split in half
8 oz. can	pizza sauce
10 slices	mozzarella cheese
¼ cup	olive oil
1 tbsp.	dried oregano

Optional your choice of:

thinly sliced mushrooms
thinly sliced green pepper
thinly sliced onions
crumbled bits of cooked bacon
small pieces of ham, pepperoni, or salami
sliced olives

Heat the oven to 450°. Arrange the split bagels on a cookie sheet and brush each of them with about 1 tsp. of the olive oil. Put them in the oven for a few minutes (4 or 5). Take them out of the oven and spread 1 tbsp. of pizza sauce on each half bagel. Then put on whatever extra ingredients you want. Cover with a slice of mozzarella cheese. Sprinkle oregano on the top along with any remaining olive oil. Put the bagels back in the oven and cook for 10 to 12 minutes, until the cheese has melted and is just beginning to brown.

VII

SUPERMARKET PIZZA

Making the Best Of It

The supermarket offers a wide variety of instant eats for the person who gets the urge for pizza and can't wait the two hours necessary to make it from scratch. Before discussing the relative merits of the instant pizzas offered in the stores, I must emphatically make one point: nothing that can be made in a few minutes is going to taste as good or be as wholesome as the labor-of-love variety. When you make your own dough and your own sauce and grate the cheeses by hand and cut up peppers and onions fresh from the garden (or from the refrigerator), you treat yourself to flavor and nutrition that cannot be put in a package. Commercial pizza manufacturers have to add preservatives to their products in order to keep them from spoiling on the shelf. They are also inclined to make up in salt and sugar what they cannot deliver in fresh flavor. So, you may "doctor up" the supermarket pizza—but you can't turn it into something it isn't.

Nevertheless, people still buy instant pizzas. Most supermarkets have an entire freezer section devoted to frozen pizza and shelf space for packaged pizzas mixes, dehydrated and canned sauce, with more ready-made pizzas in the deli section or cold cuts case. In addition to these specifically pizza products, there are pita bread, French bread, frozen bread dough, English muffins, and instant biscuit dough, all of which can be adapted for quickie pizzas.

In testing out the various pizza options, I found that within each product category, the individual brands varied widely in quality and flavor. Although I am tempted to offer my opinion on the best and the worst of the products I sampled, I will refrain from doing so. But I do strongly recommend that you sample all of the brands systematically to discover for yourself the range of quality that is available in the store. If you believe they are all about the same, you'll be very surprised.

The best principle by which to guide yourself in making instant pizza is this: The more the manufacturer has done for you, the less acceptable is the flavor of the product. Don't be fooled by the luscious-looking pictures on the packages. What you save in effort, you lose in freshness and in flavor.

I have arranged the following suggestions in descending order with respect to results, with the best first and the worst last. The biggest problem the pizza-lover must overcome in making fast pizza is finding a quality crust. You can buy a relatively good-tasting prepared sauce, but finding a pre-made or packaged pizza dough nearly as good as homemade is difficult. Nevertheless, here is how to make the best of what the commercial pizza producers have put in the stores.

FROZEN BREAD DOUGH

You can make a good-tasting genuine pizza crust from frozen bread dough. There are, however, a couple of drawbacks. First of all, you don't save time, just effort. In fact, defrosting a one pound loaf of frozen dough and letting it rise takes several hours. This doesn't help someone who gets a mad midnight craving for an instant pizza. On the other hand, it's a good method for someone who wants to take the bread dough out of the freezer in the morning and bake pizza when he or she returns home in the evening. I have also given some suggestions in the microwave section of this book on how you can defrost frozen dough in considerably less time, if you have a microwave available.

The other major drawback to commercially prepared frozen dough is that many of them include chemicals as preservatives and conditioners which you would never include if you made your own dough. If you are not a compulsive and nervous label-reader, this aspect of frozen dough may not bother you as much as it does me.

When you remove a loaf of frozen bread dough from the freezer, be sure to brush it with some oil so it does not dry out as it defrosts. Cover the dough with a clean dish towel and place it in a warm place so it can defrost and rise. The details on how long this will take will be given on the wrapper.

My experience with commercial doughs is that they do not roll out as easily as homemade dough. They don't seem to have the same degree of elasticity. Allow a whole one pound loaf of bread dough for each 12" pizza you plan to make.

Knead the dough with floured hands for a few minutes before you try to roll it out. Put flour on the board and on your rolling pin as well. One suggestion for rolling out frozen bread dough for pizza is to allow part of the dough to hang over the edge of the table as you roll the other part out. Rotate the dough frequently and always let the part that is not being rolled hang over the edge. The idea is for gravity to keep the dough from contracting back into its original shape. This method doesn't work well for me, but I pass the suggestion along because others have found it helpful. I generally alternate using a rolling pin and my hands to stretch and ease defrosted dough into shape.

The following recipe will make one 12" pizza.

1 lb.	frozen bread dough
1 cup	pizza sauce, commercially prepared or homemade
1/2 lb.	mozzarella cheese, sliced or grated
1/4 cup	grated parmesan cheese
2 tbsp.	olive oil
1 tsp.	dried oregano

(Optional garnishes: green peppers, mushrooms, onions, Canadian bacon, sausage, pepperoni, anchovies, etc.)

Allow the bread dough to defrost and rise for 4 to 6 hours covered in a warm place. Preheat the oven to 375°. Form the bread dough into a pizza crust either by rolling it out with a rolling pin or stretching it with your hands. Put the dough in a pizza pan that has been sprinkled with cornmeal.

Roll up a rim and brush the dough with 1 tbsp. of olive oil. Place the shell in the oven for 10 minutes to pre-bake slightly. Then remove the crust and turn the oven up to 400°. Spread the sauce over the crust and put on whatever optional garnishes you have selected. Cover with the cheeses and sprinkle with oregano. Dribble the remaining tbsp. of olive oil over the top and bake for another 15 to 20 minutes.

Check the pizza from time to time to be sure the crust is not getting overdone. The pizza is ready when the crust is nicely browned and the cheese is melted and bubbling.

BISCUIT DOUGH

The second-best convenience food crust can be made from the prepared biscuit dough that comes in tubes. This is not a genuine yeast-risen bread dough, but it makes a fresher and tastier crust than most other kinds of instant doughs. Biscuit dough also has the advantage of being quick to make. This is a good choice for children who are more concerned with getting the pizza into their mouths as quickly as possible than with creating an authentic dish. Kids also like the puffiness and flavor of biscuit dough crust.

One drawback to this crust is that it rises quite a lot in the oven. You may end up with a somewhat balloony-looking pizza. Be sure you bake the dough on a pan that is larger than the pizza crust in case some of the sauce spills over the edge.

Follow the instructions on the package concerning the temperature of the oven and the cooking time. I had the most success with biscuits cooked at 450°.

Like frozen bread dough, biscuit dough is not particularly easy to roll out. However, you can shape it into a pizza crust by using your hands to stretch it out initially and then finishing with a floured rolling pin.

For two 6" pizzas.

2 tubes (4.5 oz. each)	prepared biscuit dough
3/4 cup	pizza sauce, homemade or commercially prepared
1/4 lb.	grated mozzarella cheese
1/4 cup	grated parmesan or romano cheese
1 tbsp.	olive oil
1/2 tsp.	dried oregano

(Optional garnishes: green peppers, mushrooms, onions, Canadian bacon, sausage, pepperoni, anchovies, etc.)

Preheat the oven according to directions on the package. Remove the biscuit dough from the tube and knead it for a minute or so to eliminate the divisions between the individual rolls. Divide the dough into 2 equal balls. Using your hands and a rolling pin, work the dough into 2 circles about 7" in diameter. Roll up the edges to form a rim around each. Place them on a baking surface (pizza pan, baking sheet or baking tiles) that has been sprinkled with cornmeal. Be sure that the baking surface is somewhat larger than the dough so it will catch any sauce that may spill out of the pizza.

Brush the unfilled pizza shells with olive oil and place an oven-proof weight in the center of each (a pot top, or oven-proof dish). Place them in the oven and bake for half of the total baking time recommended in the instructions. Then take the dough out of the oven, remove the weights and spread half of the sauce, the garnishes, the cheeses, and the seasonings on each. Return to the oven and complete the baking.

FRENCH BREAD, PITA, BAGELS, ENGLISH MUFFINS

You can create a pizza on bread that has already been baked or partially baked to get a tasty, if not authentic, pizza crust. The results are usually very good because you assemble most of the ingredients yourself. Brush a little olive oil on the bread and bake it for five minutes or so at 375° before you add the sauce and cheese.

Use fresh tomatoes instead of sauce for the best flavor. Drain some of the liquid out of fresh tomato slices so the bread will not become soggy. Also, add some seasoning to the pizza to compensate for the herbs and spices that would have been included in the sauce. Dried oregano is the classic pizza seasoning; a little garlic powder is good, too. Experiment with basil, tarragon and other dried herbs to see what effect they have on the final result.

You will not have a rim on your bread pizza, so leave a little border around the edge when you put on the sauce. Bake the pizzas on baking sheets which will catch anything that falls off while cooking.

Cooking time will vary depending on the size and type of bread you use. You do not have to worry about underdone dough because the bread was baked before you started. Therefore, judge the doneness of the pizza by the appearance of the cheese and sauce. The cheese should be melted and the sauce bubbling. Don't let the cheese toast.

This is one of the quickest and easiest ways to make pizza and yields the greatest returns for the amount of effort extended.

PIZZA KITS AND DRY CRUST MIXES

The packaged pizza kits on the supermarket shelf may include either a dry crust mix, a crust mix and a can of sauce, or the crust mix, sauce, and a can of grated cheese. Naturally, you pay the most for the greatest convenience, and sometimes the cost is in flavor as well as in dollars and cents. The problem with buying a complete pizza kit is that the best can of sauce and the best dry crust mix are not necessarily in the same kit. Of course, this is a matter of personal preference and you should sample the products that are available in your area and decide which ones suit your taste. However, I recommend buying the crust mix and the prepared sauce separately and adding your own fresh sliced or grated cheese. Pizza kits, in general, produce tastier pizza for the price than a frozen pizza. It takes a few minutes to prepare, but it's easy enough for a child to do without any difficulty.

The dry mixes make better-tasting crusts than I expected, but they really were not in the same class as frozen bread dough or prepared biscuit dough. You can buy packaged hot roll mix or buttermilk biscuit mix as well as products specifically made for pizza. Instructions for pizza crusts are usually included on the boxes of the roll and biscuit mixes. The dough that you make from a dry mix is very sticky. You can't roll it out with a rolling pin, you have to shape the crust in the pan with your fingers. Instead of using cornmeal on the pan to keep the crust from sticking, you generally have to use butter or oil. Furthermore, you can't use this kind of dough to form a top crust as you can with an elastic, homemade dough or a frozen bread dough.

You can only improve a packaged pizza by adding fresh ingredients to what you buy in the box. Put on your own cheese, garnishes, seasonings, anything that is fresh. If you use a dry crust mix, your favorite prepared sauce and some cheese and garnishes from your refrigerator, you can make a tasty super-quick snack at midnight, during t.v. commercials, or when the kids come home from school.

FROZEN AND PRE-MADE CRUSTS

As I mentioned previously, a dry mix will give you a tastier crust than a pre-made or frozen one. Both the texture and the flavor of the mixes that I have tried are better than crusts that have been allowed to sit on a shelf or in the freezer for weeks (or even longer). Another drawback to prepared crusts is that they do not have a rim to keep in the sauce and the cheese. I don't know why manufacturers make flat pizza crusts; it must be a matter of packaging.

In spite of my reservations about prepared pizza crusts, I still think they are better than the crust you get on a fully assembled frozen pizza. The flavor and the texture of a frozen crust will improve somewhat if you allow it to defrost before baking. Because commercially prepared crusts are thin, defrosting does not take very long, usually only 20 to 30 minutes.

Brush the dough with a little oil and spread sauce on top. You can't put as much sauce on a frozen crust as you would on other kinds because there is no rim. In fact, you must leave a little border around the edge with no sauce at all to prevent it from spilling in the oven. You have some control over the texture of the final product. If you want a crisp crust, bake it directly on the rack of your oven or on a baking stone or tile. If you like a softer crust, use a baking sheet.

When you use a prepared crust, the strength of your pizza will have to be in the ingredients you add from your own refrigerator. Use a tasty sauce, either commercial or homemade, and lots of fresh garnishes. Green peppers have an especially desirable flavor when they are sliced fresh and added. Use freshly grated cheese, but not so much that it will spill over the edge. Season with oregano and garlic powder and bake according to the instructions on the package.

FROZEN FRENCH OR ITALIAN BREAD PIZZA

Some frozen pizza manufacturers are now making frozen French bread pizza or frozen Italian bread pizza. These breads make a better base for frozen pizza than the usual thin layer of flavorless dough that you get in conventional frozen pizza. The drawbacks to the French bread type are: you may not like the sauce that the manufacturer provides and you pay an excessive amount for what you get.

It makes more sense to me to keep some French or Italian bread frozen in the freezer, a good pizza sauce on your shelf and mozzarella cheese in the refrigerator. You can get a lot more French bread pizza for your money and better flavor if you keep the ingredients separate until the last minute and combine them yourself.

Buy a long loaf of French or Italian bread and slice it into the size you will want before you wrap it and put it in the freezer. You can then take it out and put a pizza together quickly whenever hunger strikes.

Bread defrosts very quickly because it is so porous. You can hasten the process even further by putting the frozen slices in a warm oven for a few minutes.

When the bread is defrosted, brush it with some oil, spoon sauce onto it, add garnishes, slices of cheese and dried herbs. If you do for yourself what the manufacturer has done for you, the profits will be yours--both in flavor and in dollars.

FROZEN PIZZA

Whole frozen pizzas are the most convenient of the quickie pizzas. The texture and flavor of the crust and sauce do not improve by being frozen together and kept in the freezer case. I am a firm believer that the crust and the sauce should be put together only at the last minute. Not only do you pay in loss of flavor, you pay excessively in dollars for extra trimmings such as sausage, green pepper, mushrooms or extra cheese. All of these things should be added fresh from the refrigerator for the best flavor and greatest economy.

The most lavish frozen pizzas cost close to $6.00. For much less money and only a little effort you can make a better-tasting pizza by combining a crust made from biscuit dough, a good prepared sauce, and your own fresh garnishes, herbs and cheese.

If you still want to use a whole frozen pizza, here are some ways to make the best of what you get. Experiment with the various brands that are available in your local stores. See which has the best-tasting sauce and the most acceptable crust. Don't buy the fancy pizzas--just the plain cheese, sauce and crust combination. When you have found the pizza that suits your taste, use it as a base and doctor it up.

The pizza will improve if you defrost it for 30 minutes before baking. While you are letting it thaw out, you can cut up some fresh garnishes to put on top. Also add any left-over bits of cheese you have in the refrigerator and crumble dried herbs on the top.

Bake according to the directions on the package. If you like a soft crust, use a baking sheet; for a crisper crust, bake directly on the oven rack or a baking stone.

PREPARED SAUCES

There are some good, ready-made sauces on the market that you can keep on your shelf for making a quick pizza in the middle of the night. Do some comparison tasting to find the sauce that suits your palate. All sauces do **not** taste alike. Check the ingredients on the label when you are doing your taste tests. Be sure that the flavor they deliver comes from fresh, natural ingredients--and not laboratory simulations.

Pizza sauce should be thicker than spaghetti sauce. If you want to adapt your favorite spaghetti sauce to use on pizzas, thicken it either with some tomato paste or by gently cooking some of the liquid out of it.

I never buy prepared sauce with extra ingredients, such as meat or mushrooms. If you want to make a meat sauce, brown ground meat in a frying pan and then add the prepared sauce to it and simmer for 10 minutes. You will undoubtedly put in better and more meat than the sauce company. Similarly, for mushroom sauce, wipe eight to 10 mushrooms clean with a damp cloth or a mushroom brush, slice them thin and saute them in butter and vegetable oil for four minutes. Then pour the prepared sauce over them and simmer for 10 minutes.

Anything you add fresh to a prepared sauce will improve it. You can saute onions and garlic and then pour the sauce over them and simmer. Or add fresh green peppers, carrots, zuccini, eggplant, and so on. On the other hand, if you are going to spend time doctoring up a prepared sauce, you can just as easily make your own sauce from scratch. And when you make your own sauce you have complete control over the seasonings and eliminate artificial ingredients, additives and extenders. So, before you go too far improving upon a commercially prepared sauce, think about how easy it is to make your own homemade sauce.

POWDERED SPAGHETTI SAUCE MIXES

I have not found a dry mix for spaghetti sauce that I can honestly say is satisfactory. All you are getting in the envelope, it seems, is sugar, salt, starchy thickeners and flavorings (some of them artificial). The resulting flavor is not wholesome, fresh or delicate, but heavy, overly spiced and artificial. Furthermore, the dry package is not particularly convenient. You have to add tomatoes (in the form of tomato paste), shortening and water and simmer for 10 to 20 minutes. It is much easier and the flavor is simply better if you open a good can or jar of prepared sauce. Many prepared sauces do not have additives and artificial ingredients.

Nonetheless, I have two suggestions to adapt dry sauce mixes for use on pizza. First of all, to create a thicker sauce which will not make the pizza crust soggy, add only half of the water recommended on the package. Then cook the sauce over a very low flame to keep it from burning. If the mix you use is very spicy, reserve part of the contents of the package. In other words, use half of the water recommended, all of the tomato paste and shortening, and half to three-quarters of the dry mix.

Another idea that will give you a chunky pizza with fresher flavor is to use a large can (28 oz.) of whole Italian plum tomatoes instead of the tomato paste. Drain all of the liquid out of the can and puncture the tomatoes so you can drain the liquid from them as well. Put the drained tomatoes in a saucepan with the dry mix and the shortening. Don't add any water at all. Chop up the tomatoes with a spoon as the sauce cooks. The sauce should be thick and chunky when it is done.

ADDITIONAL IDEAS

Pizzeria dough: If you are a regular customer at your local pizzeria, you can probably negotiate a deal with the owner so that you can buy fresh pizza dough from them when you want to make your pizza at home. If you are a **really** good customer they may even give you dough from time to time as a gesture of good will. This is, of course, the easiest way to get great homemade pizza.

Cheese bag: Julia Child does this--and so should we. Save little scraps and ends of cheese in a bag in the refrigerator. When you need some cheese to put on the top of pizza, grate all of the little pieces and use them together. Cheese flavors generally blend well, so you needn't worry about the randomness of the combination.

Par-baked pizza: Many pizzerias sell their products in partially baked form. Keep them in your freezer and complete the baking in your own oven. These locally-made pizzas are generally better than the frozen pizzas in the supermarket. They are made in smaller batches, kept for shorter periods of time, and have less opportunity to deteriorate in transit. To make your own par-baked pizzas, see the section on freezers in Chapter VIII.

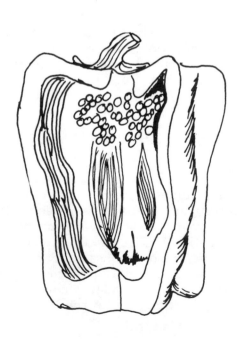

VIII

THE WAVE OF THE FUTURE

Using the Little Helpers Mama Never Had: Food Processor, Microwave and Convection Ovens, Freezer and Barbecue

New kitchen appliances are always being invented and presented to the public for approval. A few that have appeared in recent years have had a profound impact on the way Americans cook. Foremost among the revolutionary new appliances have been the microwave oven and the food processor. Americans have less and less time to spend in the kitchen, but are becoming more and more interested in food and its preparation. Both the microwave and the food processor substantially reduce the time necessary to prepare meals. Even the busy career person need not abandon his or her love for homemade gourmet-quality food with a microwave oven and a food processor in the kitchen.

The combination of freezer and microwave allows delicious homemade food to be prepared when time is abundant and then stored for almost instant defrosting and cooking when time is scarce.

Convection ovens are available for home use now, too. They are not really new, having been used in hotels and commercial kitchens for years. Only recently, however, have private home owners been able to enjoy the advantages of convection cooking. Having mastered the few easy principles of convection cooking, you can make your old favorite recipes with exciting new results--and in less time.

The barbecue is not a time-saver, but it is a wonderful American cooking tradition, as much a sign of summer as the robin is of spring. The advent of the kettle barbecue has made all kinds of food suitable for outdoor cooking that used to be confined to the kitchen. Among these newcomers to the barbecue is the hero of this book: Pizza!

FOOD PROCESSOR

The food processor can make almost every step of pizza-making quicker and easier. It can knead the dough, grate the cheese, slice the garnishes, and puree the sauce. For one 12" pizza.

Dough

2 cups	unbleached all-purpose flour
1 pkg.	dry yeast
½ tsp.	salt
1 tsp.	sugar
2 tbsp.	olive oil
¾ cup	warm water

Stir the yeast and the sugar into ¼ cup of warm water and set it aside for 5 minutes. Sift the flour and salt into the processor bowl with the steel mixing blade or dough hook. Add the oil, ½ cup of warm water and the yeast mixture. If your machine has a dough hook, follow the machine directions for kneading. If you are using a steel mixing blade, use the on/off method and knead the dough until it forms a small, elastic ball. Remove the dough from the processor and place it in a greased bowl, brush with a little oil and cover with a clean dish towel. Place the bowl in a warm, draft-free place for 1½ hours.

Tomato Sauce

1 tbsp.	olive oil
1 small	onion
1 small clove	garlic
1 cup	Italian plum tomatoes, drained
1 tbsp.	tomato paste
¼ tsp.	dried basil
¼ tsp.	dried tarragon
½ tsp.	dried oregano
¼ tsp.	brown sugar
½ tsp.	salt
	pepper

Heat the oil in a saute pan. Place the onion and garlic in the processor with the steel blade and mince with the on/off method. Remove and saute the minced onion and garlic for 5 minutes. If you want your sauce pureed, put the drained tomatoes, tomato paste and seasonings in the bowl and process until the sauce is thick and smooth. Add the tomato sauce to the saute pan and cook for 30 minutes over low heat. The sauce should just barely simmer.

Cheese

Grate ⅛ lb. of parmesan or romano cheese and ½ lb. of mozzarella cheese with the shredder or grater attachment.

Garnishes

Slice mushrooms, green peppers, onions, pepperoni, olives and other garnishes with the slicing attachment.

To assemble the pizza

When the dough has risen for 1½ hours, preheat the oven to 450°. Roll out the dough and place it on a pizza pan, baking sheet or baking stone that has been sprinkled with cornmeal. Roll up a rim and brush the dough with olive oil. Spread the sauce on the dough and distribute the cheeses and garnishes over the top. Dribble a little more olive oil over the pizza and bake for 20 to 25 minutes until the crust is golden brown.

MICROWAVE OVEN

Baking bread dough is **not** one of the things that a microwave does better than a conventional oven. There are some products on the market that claim to be able to brown pizza crusts, but I found them unsatisfactory. The microwave pizza stone that I tried had to be preheated for seven and a half minutes. After the preheating period, the pizza (frozen or homemade) cooks for about five minutes, and it has to be turned at least once. The savings in time over a conventional oven is not substantial and the results are inferior. A piece of cardboard under a homemade pizza did just as well without preheating and took the same amount of time.

If you want to make homemade pizza in the microwave, it will take four and a half to five minutes to cook. Don't put sliced peppers, mushrooms, or onions on until the cooking time is half over. When you open the oven to turn the pizza, place the garnishes on top. The crust will puff up and cook, but it will not brown. Although the flavor is good, it is not exactly the same as crust cooked in old-fashioned ovens.

On the other hand, in less than 15 minutes you can make a wonderful meat-crust pizza in the microwave for a great dinner treat. The microwave allows the vegetables to keep all of their fresh flavor. To serve eight.

MEAT-CRUST PIZZA

1 lb.	lean hamburger meat
2 slices	whole wheat bread
½ cup	whipping cream
1 cup	homemade pizza sauce
2 cups	grated mozzarella cheese
½ cup	grated parmesan cheese
6 mushrooms	wiped clean and sliced
1 small	green pepper, sliced
1 cup	sliced Italian salad onion

Soak the slices of whole wheat bread in the cream until they are soft and can be mashed. Add the hamburger meat and combine thoroughly. Line two, 8″ glass pie plates with the meat mixture to form a crust. Cook them one at a time in the microwave oven. Each should cook for 3 minutes; turn the pie plate after 1½ minutes. When the crust has cooked for 3 minutes, take it out of the oven and discard any fat that has melted off. Divide the sauce and the cheese between the pies. Cook each pie for 5 minutes. After the first 2½ minutes, turn the pie plate and add the peppers, onions, and mushrooms. When the first pie is done, take it out of the oven and let it rest for 5 minutes. Meanwhile, cook the second pie. Cut and serve the first one while the second is resting out of the oven.

Defrosting in the Microwave

The microwave can be of great assistance in preparing homemade pizza by enabling you to defrost frozen batches of sauce and dough rapidly. Sauce frozen in one cup containers can be defrosted in only a few minutes. Even more remarkable is the oven's ability to defrost dough while only operating the oven for a total of eight minutes.

To defrost a one pound loaf of frozen bread dough, first put three cups of water in a large measuring cup and place it in the oven. Set the timer for seven minutes and boil the water. Put the frozen dough on a plate and place it in the oven with the cup of water. Turn on the oven for 30 seconds and leave the oven closed for 20 minutes. Then turn the oven on for another 30 seconds and leave the dough in it for another 20 minutes. The dough should now be defrosted. In less than an hour, you have defrosted dough that usually takes from four to six hours to thaw. With the microwave, making up several loaves of dough and saving them for later use becomes an economical and convenient practice.

CONVECTION OVEN

The convection oven circulates hot air by means of a fan. Commercial kitchens have used convection cooking for a long time, and it is now available for home use. The uniform heat of convection cooking provides ideal conditions for baking bread. What's good for bread is also good for pizza. The convection oven makes a beautiful crust and cooks pizza in less time than a conventional oven.

Home models of convection ovens are generally smaller than traditional ovens. Most of them will not accommodate a large pizza pan. I had success making several individual pizzas at once in the oven, baking each one on its own baking tile. I also used a 9″ cake pan to make an outstanding deep-dish pizza. The pizzas baked on the tiles bake more quickly than the deep-dish pizza because so much more surface area is exposed to the air circulating through the oven.

The general rule for convection baking is to subtract 50° to 75° from the recommended baking temperature and shorten the baking time by five to 10 minutes. Baking time will vary, of course, with the size of the pizza and the thickness of the crust. Let the general rule be your guide, but keep an eye on the pizza as it bakes. Judge when the pizza is done by the appearance of the crust and the filling. Any of the recipes in the preceding chapters can be made with excellent results in a convection oven.

Frozen and par-baked pizzas benefit from the circulated heat in convection cooking, too. Again, size may limit the use of your oven. If you make your own frozen pizzas, they can be scaled down to match the size of your oven.

FREEZER

Make your own frozen pizza that can be taken out anytime for unexpected company or very special snacks. Partially baked pizzas will keep beautifully in the freezer, but they generally don't get a chance to stay there too long. When your family and friends know you have homemade pizza on ice, you'll have daily requests and a long line of kids queued up at your kitchen door waiting to eat.

When you are making pizzas to freeze, keep them about 10" in diameter. The crust should be relatively thick in order to provide a stable framework for the pizza. I like to assemble the pizzas on baking tiles or pizza stones outside of the oven. Cover the unfilled pizza shells with a clean cloth and let them rise for 15 minutes before putting the sauce and garnishes on the dough. Brush the dough well with olive oil and bake for 10 minutes less than the recipe indicates.

When you take the pizzas out of the oven, slide them off of the baking tiles immediately and cool them on racks. Leaving the pizzas on the tiles prolongs the cooking and the pizzas will cool too slowly. After the pizzas have cooled, wrap them tightly in freezer wrap and put them in the freezer.

You will get the best results with par-baked pizzas if you defrost them for about an hour before you finish cooking them. However, if you are in a hurry, put them straight in the oven without defrosting. Cook them in an oven that has been preheated to 400°. They will take at least 20 minutes to heat up. If you have not defrosted them, they will take longer to get hot in the middle. The exact cooking time depends on the size of the pizza and the thickness of the crust. The best way to find out if the pizza is fully cooked is to stick your finger in the center. In fact, I know of no other way.

The convection oven reheats par-baked pizzas especially well. Place them directly on the racks with no pan underneath. The hot air will circulate evenly around the pizza and cook the bottom at the same rate as the top and sides.

BARBECUE

Imagine your friends' faces when you invite them over for a barbecue and pull a home-baked pizza out of the grill! They will be delighted--and so will you. Use any of the recipes given in the preceding chapters to prepare the pizza. Start the coals when the dough has been rising for 30 minutes. It will take about an hour for the fire to be ready, just in time to roll out the dough.

Pile up the charcoal in the center of the grill. Light it and allow it to burn for about 20 minutes until each piece is at least partially ash-gray. Then spread the coals into two equal piles at the sides of the kettle and put the grill on top. (A gas barbecue should be set at "high.") Put a baking stone or baking tiles on the grill and place the hood over the barbecue. Heat the stone for a half hour over the coals.

When the dough has risen for 90 minutes, roll it out and make a pizza shell slightly smaller than your baking surface. Place the dough on a pizza paddle (peel) that has been sprinkled with cornmeal. Put a cloth over the unfilled pizza shell and let it rise for 15 minutes. Then brush the dough with olive oil, spread sauce on it and cover the top with garnishes and cheese. Dribble more olive oil over the pizza and take it out to the barbecue.

Sprinkle cornmeal on the preheated stone just before you put the pizza on it. Slide the pizza off the paddle by shaking the paddle from side to side. The pizza will move slowly forward onto the stone. Replace the cover and let the pizza cook for 15 minutes. Check it every 5 minutes thereafter. When the crust is golden brown, lift the pizza off the stone with the paddle.

The outdoor oven will stay hot for a long time, so you can bake several pizzas in a row for a hungry crowd.

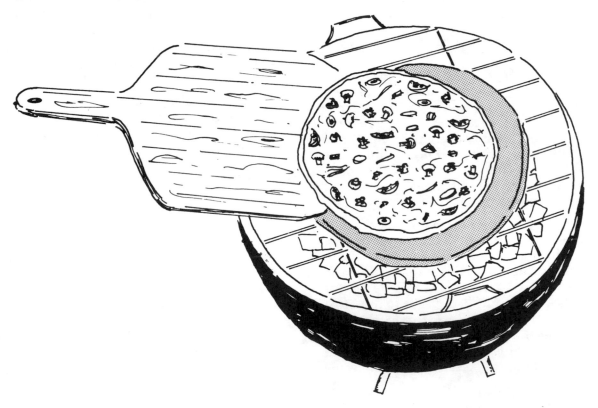

IX
TOOLS OF THE TRADE

Utensils For Pizza Making

DEEP DISH PIZZA PAN

Available in various sizes from 8" to 14" in diameter and 1½" to 2" inches in depth. Most pizzerias use tin-plated steel pans, but aluminum pans are also available. Tin plate forms a very strong alloy with steel to produce a better, more even heating surface than aluminum. Disposable foil pizza pans are also available in many supermarkets, but ecological considerations make them undesirable.

THIN-CRUST PIZZA PAN

Available in various diameters and materials comparable to the deep dish pans, but ranging from a slightly raised rim to a 1" depth.

PERFORATED PIZZA PAN

These pans have holes perforated in the bottom to permit more heat to reach the bottom of the pizza, thus creating a uniformly crisp crust.

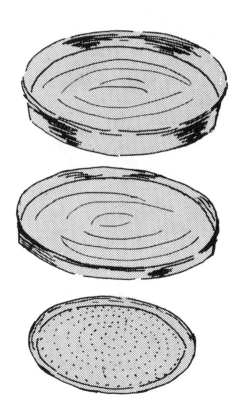

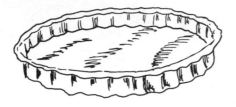

CLAY BAKERS

Clay baking, which is as old as man's use of fire, is experiencing an extraordinary renaissance. Clay pie pans and quiche pans can be very effectively adapted for baking pizzas. A deep dish clay baking pan is now also available. Clay bakers have the advantage of producing total, even heat distribution and moisture absorption. This produces crisp crusts.

BAKING PLATES AND BAKING TILES

Available in a variety of shapes and sizes, this highly fired natural stoneware produces a very even heating surface and absorbs moisture, producing crispy crusts. Julia Child, Marcella Hazan and James Beard all praise the virtues of baking with tiles. Most gourmet and department stores sell baking tiles. If you buy tiles from a quarry, make certain that they are safe to cook on and free of toxic contaminants.

You may bake directly on the tiles, but even when you're not using them, leaving them in the oven will help to evenly distribute and hold a steady temperature. Metal pans may be placed on the tiles and will benefit from the tiles' even heating properties.

Some baking plates are sold with a rack which allows you to take the stone directly from the oven to the table. The stone retains heat for a considerable time after it has been removed from the oven, and pizza will be kept warm while being served from the stone.

PIZZA PEELS

These wooden boards or paddles are technically called "make up peels." Pizzeria chefs construct pizzas on peels and slide them into and out of pizza ovens. The edges of the peels are finely tapered to permit scooping the pizza out of the ovens.

PIZZA CUTTERS

Cutters come in a variety of sizes and at widely varying prices. Two important features to consider are a stainless steel wheel and a thumb guard.

PIZZA SCISSORS

Pizza is often easier to cut with a scissors. Look for a scissors with an offset handle and a stainless steel blade.

PAN GRABBER

This clever gadget is really a detachable handle which is helpful for removing pans with beaded edges from hot ovens and carrying them to the table.

ROLLING PINS

Available in three basic shapes and a variety of weights and lengths:

French pin: A cylinder without handles that lets you feel the thickness and texture of the dough as it is rolled out.

Tapered pin: Small in diameter this pin tapers to both ends. It is very useful for rolling out circles for pizza doughs.

American pin: This all-purpose pin moves independently from the handles, requiring less effort to roll out the dough.

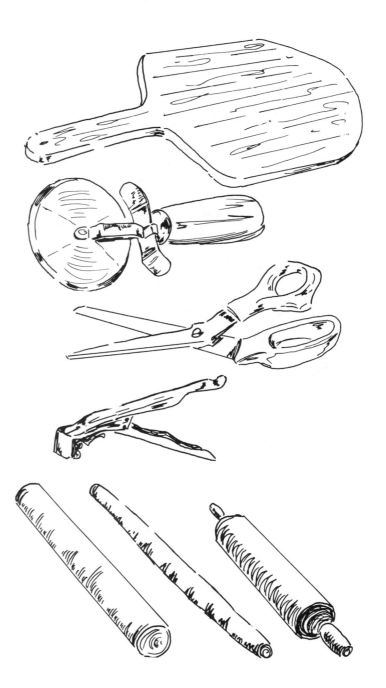

YEAST THERMOMETER

A handly gadget that takes the guesswork out of preparing a yeast dough, allowing you to add water at the correct temperature to the yeast.

PASTRY BRUSH

Use this to glaze doughs and to brush oil on the dough.

DOUGH HOOK

This attachment for mixers takes the hard work out of mixing and kneading dough.

MUSHROOM BRUSH

Mushrooms will not saute properly if they have been washed, because they absorb too much water. A mushroom brush will clean the mushrooms without allowing water to soak into them.

CHEESE GRATER

If you don't have the luxury of a food processor, a cheese grater is an absolutely necessary tool. They are available in both cylindrical and straight styles. Cylindrical graters usually grate hard romano and parmesan cheeses more easily than the straight variety, saving you from scraped knuckles.

RESOURCES

Sassafras Enterprises, Inc. supplies a full line of pizza making equipment to the retail trade. For a list of stores near you write:
Sassafras Enterprises, Inc.
P.O. Box 461
Evanston, IL 60204

INDEX

- A -

Anchovy 28, 29, 30, 68
Apples 48
Artichoke 41
Avocado 40, 60

- B -

Bagel 80, 84
Baking tiles 19
Barbecue 93-94
Bleu cheese 45
Brie cheese 45, 66
Burag b'jeben 55

- C -

Calzone 18, 44
Camembert cheese 45, 66
Cheddar cheese 40, 48, 66
Chicago-style deep-dish pizza 17
Chicory 30
Chili 40
Colby cheese 38
Convection oven 92-93
Cornish pasties 59
Cottage cheese 55, 57, 62
Cream cheese 62, 65, 66
Crust
  Frozen and pre-made 85

- D -

Deep-dish pizza 17, 40, 72
Double-crust pizza 17-18, 35
Dough 13
  Baking soda 23
  Basic pizza dough 14
  Biscuit 83
  Brioche 23
  Buttermilk 21

Cheese and onion 22
Frozen 82
Gougere 46, 58
Pate brisee 63
Pita 24
Phyllo 55, 61, 66
Pumpernickel 24
Rye 21
Slow rising 22
Spinach and ricotta 20
Whole wheat 20

- E -

Egg, shirred 46
Egg roll wrappers 47
Eggplant 37
Emmentaler cheese 55
English muffins 80, 84
Envueltos de aguacate 60

- F -

Felafel 64
Feta cheese 55, 61
Food processor 90-91
Freezer 93
French bread 51, 54, 55, 84, 85

- G -

Gebackene kasebrotchen 55
Gibanica 66
Gougere aux epinards 58
Gruyere cheese 38, 49, 50, 55
Guacamole 60

- H -

Hae kung 65
Hot dogs 75, 76, 77

- K -

Kasari cheese 66
Kaseschnitten mit champignons .. 54
Khachapuri 67

- M -

Macaroni 79
Mantarh borek 66
Matzah 77
Meatballs 36
Microwave oven 91-92
Monterey jack cheese 38, 60
Mozzarella, history of 9, 10
Munster cheese 67

- O -

Okono mi-yaki 56

- P -

Parmesan, history of 10
Pesto 31
Pierogi 62
Pissaladiere 10, 68
Pita 24, 64, 72, 84
Pizza
  Casserole 79
  Chicago-style deep-dish 17, 40
  Double-crust 17-18
  Dough, basic 14
  Frozen 86
  History 9-11
  Mixes 84
  Nutritional value 11-12
  Par-baked 88, 93
  Recipes
    A la hot dog 76
    Antipasto 44
    Apple and cheddar cheese 48

INDEX

Bagels 80
Barbecue 93-94
Biscuit 83
Bleu cheese 45
Capricciosa 28
Chili 40
Deli 34
Di scammero 30
Eggplant 37
Elegant seafood 50
Festive sausage 32
Florentine 41
Four cheese 35
Frozen bread dough 82
Frutti di mare 39
Gardener's no-flour 34
Hawaiian sweet and sour 38
Hot dog 76
Low calorie 39
Margherita 28
Matzah 77
Meat crust 92
Meatball 36
Mexican 38
Miniature deep-dish 72
Napoletana 29
Pesto 31
Pissaladiere 68
Pita 72
Pompeii 29
Rolls, egg 47
Rustica 33
Sausage 32
Scammero 30
Seafood 35, 39, 50
Shirred egg 46
Shrimp, double crust 35
Skillet 41

Smorgasbord 49
Strawberry shortcake 78
Stuffed, spinach and ricotta .. 33
Sweet and sour 38
Valentine's Day 74
Sauce 27
Stuffed pocket 16, 33
Thick-crust 16
Thin-crust 15
Prosciutto 28, 33, 44
Provolone cheese 35
Pyriszhky 68

· Q ·

Quiche 62

- R -

Ricotta cheese 20, 33, 35

- S -

Sandwich
  Gebackene Kasebrotchen 55
  Hero 51
  Kaseschnitten mit champignons 54
  Pizza bagels 80
  Pizza burgers 80
  Pizza dogs 75
Sauce
  Prepared 86-87
  Tomato 27
Sausage 32, 33, 47, 49
Scallops 50
Shrimp 35, 38, 39, 50, 65
Skillet 41
Smorgasbord 49
Spanakopita 61
Spinach 58, 61
  Dough with ricotta 20
  Stuffed pizza rustica 33

Strawberries 78
Stuffed pizza pocket 16, 33
Swiss cheese 46, 49, 54, 55, 63

- T -

Tiles, baking 19, 93, 94, 96
Tofu 37
Tomato
  History 10
  Sauce 27
Tortillas 60
Tuna 30, 39, 44

- U -

Utensils 95-98

- V -

Vatrushki 57
Vegetarian wedge 51

- Y -

Yogurt 57, 78

- Z -

Zuccini 34